Lao

lonely planet

phrasebooks
and
Joe Cummings

Lao phrasebook
3rd edition – March 2008

Published by
Lonely Planet Publications Pty Ltd ABN 36 005 607 983
90 Maribyrnong St, Footscray, Victoria 3011, Australia

Lonely Planet Offices
Australia Locked Bag 1, Footscray, Victoria 3011
USA 150 Linden St, Oakland CA 94607
UK 2nd floor, 186 City Rd, London, EC1V 2NT

Cover illustration
River Cruise by Cara Smith

ISBN 978 1 74059 492 9

10 9 8 7 6 5 4 3 2

Printed through Colorcraft Ltd, Hong Kong
Printed in China

acknowledgments

about the author

After investing most of his youth strangling Stratocasters in dark bars, Joe Cummings ran away from home with the Peace Corps and discovered South-East Asia. Returning to his native USA, he earned meagre but steady cash as a professional student for several years, gaining two master's degrees, one in South-East Asian Studies/Thai Language and another in Applied Linguistics. He has also worked as a translator/interpreter of Thai, a Lao bilingual consultant in the USA and as a tour guide in Laos. Along the way, Joe hit the road for LP, writing the first editions of LP's *Thailand* and *Laos* guides, which he continues to update regularly. He has also authored LP's *Thai phrasebook*, *World Food: Thailand* and *Buddhist Stupas of Asia: The Shape of Perfection*. Joe visits Laos frequently from his home base in Thailand.

from the author

I'm much indebted to a Lao friend who helped with the Lao script for this phrasebook, but who wished not to be mentioned by name. Thanks also to Steven Schipani, who facilitated many exchanges. For logistical support, I thank Oliver Bandmann of Baan Khily Gallery in Luang Prabang.

from the publisher

This expedition was mounted by Sally Steward, Peter D'Onghia and Ingrid Seebus in its early days, then commandeered by Jim Jenkin. Karina Coates and Karin Vidstrup Monk planned the imminent stages of departure and made short work of the dense jungle, thus guiding the team to new territory. Dogsbody Ben Handicott edited the scribe's account. Yukiyoshi Kamimura was expedition artist from cover to cover, and also charted the layout of the whole affair. Bruce Evans lent a learned eye to the itinerary, Sophie Putman was the invaluable trip jack-of-all-trades (master of many), Natasha Velleley plotted the map, Bibiana Jaramillo made sure it was all recorded in the correct typeface and Fabrice Rocher, another crazy Frenchman, provided his sparkling eyes and guaranteed a stylish, timely arrival at destination. Special thanks to Manivone Watson for the creation of the Sustainable Travel section.

make the most of this phrasebook ...

Anyone can speak another language! It's all about confidence. Don't worry if you can't remember your school language lessons or if you've never learnt a language before. Even if you learn the very basics (on the inside covers of this book), your travel experience will be the better for it. You have nothing to lose and everything to gain when the locals hear you making an effort.

finding things in this book

For easy navigation, this book is in sections. The Pronunciation and Grammar chapters are the ones you'll thumb through time and again. The Getting Around and Accommodation chapters cover basic travel situations like catching transport and finding a bed. The Meeting People chapter gives you conversational phrases and the ability to express opinions – so you can get to know people. Food has a section all of its own: gourmets and vegetarians are covered and local dishes feature. The Health and Emergencies chapters equip you with health and police phrases, just in case. Use the comprehensive Index to find everything easily. Otherwise, check the traveller's Dictionary for the word you need.

being understood

Throughout this book you'll see coloured phrases on each page. They're phonetic guides to help you pronounce the language. Start with them to get a feel for how the language sounds. The Pronunciation chapter will explain more, but you can be confident that if you read the coloured phrase, you'll be understood.

communication tips

Body language, ways of doing things, sense of humour – all have a role to play in every culture. The aside boxes included throughout this phrasebook give you useful cultural and linguistic information that will help you communicate with the locals and enrich your travel experience.

CONTENTS

lao

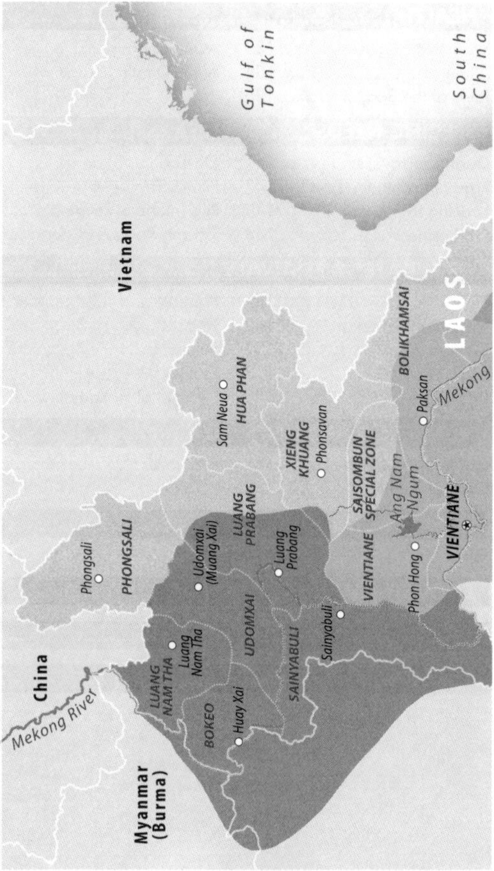
Vietnam
Gulf of Tonkin
South China
China
Mekong River
Myanmar (Burma)
LAOS
PHONGSALI
Phongsali
LUANG NAM THA
Luang Nam Tha
BOKEO
Huay Xai
UDOMXAI
Udomxai (Muang Xai)
LUANG PRABANG
Luang Prabang
SAINYABULI
Sainyabuli
HUA PHAN
Sam Neua
XIENG KHUANG
Phonsavan
SAISOMBUN SPECIAL ZONE
Ang Nam Ngum
VIENTIANE
Phon Hong
VIENTIANE
BOLIKHAMSAI
Paksan
Mekong

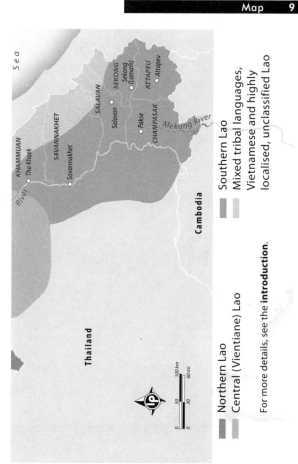

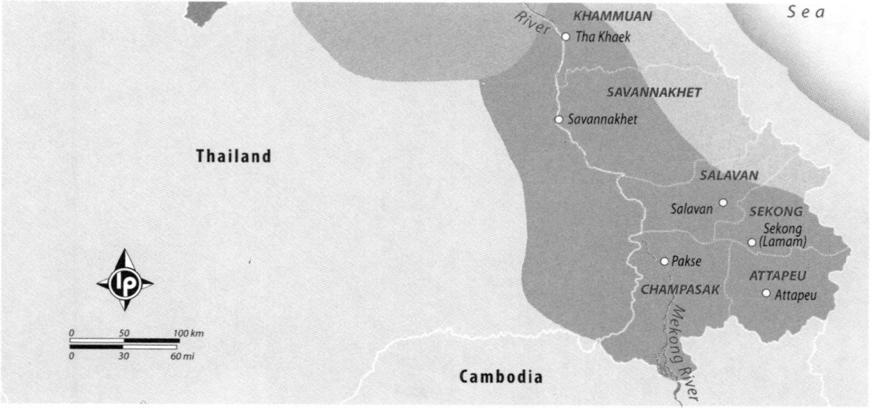

Northern Lao
Central (Vientiane) Lao

For more details, see the **introduction**.

Southern Lao
Mixed tribal languages, Vietnamese and highly localised, unclassified Lao

INTRODUCTION

The official language of the Lao People's Democratic Republic (LPDR) is Lao as spoken and written in Vientiane. As an official language, it has successfully become the lingua franca between all Lao and non-Lao ethnic groups in Laos. Of course, native Lao is spoken with differing tonal accents and with slightly differing vocabularies as you move from one part of the country to the next, especially in a north to south direction. But it is the Vientiane dialect that is most widely understood.

Modern Lao linguists recognise four basic dialects within the country: Vientiane Lao; Northern Lao (spoken in Sainyabuli, Bokeo, Udomxai, Phongsali, Luang Nam Tha and Luang Prabang); North-Eastern Lao (Xieng Khuang, Hua Phan), Central Lao (Khammuan, Bolikhamsai); and Southern Lao (Champasak, Salavan, Savannakhet, Attapeu, Sekong). Each of these can be further divided into subdialects; a distinction between the Lao spoken in the neighbouring provinces of Xieng Khuang and Hua Phan, for example, is readily apparent to those who know Lao well.

All dialects of Lao are members of the Thai half of the Thai-Kadai family of languages and are closely related to languages spoken in Thailand, northern Myanmar and pockets of China's Yunnan Province. Standard Lao is indeed close enough to Standard Thai (as spoken in central Thailand) that, for native speakers, the two are mutually intelligible. In fact, virtually all speakers of Lao living in the Mekong River Valley can easily understand spoken Thai, since the bulk of the television and radio they listen to is broadcast from Thailand. Among educated Lao, written Thai is also easily understood, in spite of the fact that the two scripts differ (to about the same degree that the Greek and Roman scripts differ). This is because many of the textbooks used at the college and university level in Laos are actually Thai texts.

Even closer to Standard Lao are Thailand's Northern and North-Eastern Thai dialects. North-Eastern Thai (also called Isan) is virtually 100% Lao in vocabulary and intonation; in fact there are more Lao speakers living in Thailand than in Laos. Hence if you're travelling to Laos after a spell in Thailand (especially the north-east), you should be able to put whatever you learned in Thailand to good use in Laos. It doesn't work as well in the opposite direction; native Thais can't always understand Lao since they've had less exposure.

ABBREVIATIONS USED IN THIS BOOK

adj	adjective	pl	plural
adv	adverb	prep	preposition
conj	conjunction	sg	singular
lit	literal translation	v	verb
n	noun		

The rendering of Lao words into Roman script is a major problem, as many Lao sounds, especially certain vowels, do not occur in English. The problem is compounded by the fact that, because of Laos' colonial history, transcribed words most commonly seen in Laos are based on the colonial French system of transliteration, which bears little relation to the way an English speaker would usually choose to write a Lao word.

Take, for example, the capital of Laos, Vientiane. The Lao pronunciation, following a fairly logical English transliteration, would be Wieng Chan (some might hear it more as Wieng Jan). The French don't have a written consonant that corresponds to 'w', so they chose to use a 'v' to represent all 'w' sounds, even though the 'v' sound in Lao is closer to an English 'w'. The same goes for 'ch' (or 'j'), which for the French was best rendered 'ti-'; hence Wieng Chan comes out 'Vientiane' in the French transliteration. The 'e' is added so that the final 'n' sound isn't partially lost, as it is in French words ending with 'n'. This latter phenomenon also happens with words like **lâan** (ລ້ານ, million) as in Lan Xang, which most French speakers would write as 'Lane', a spelling that leads most English speakers to pronounce this word like the 'lane' in 'Penny Lane' (which is way off base).

As there is no official method of transliterating Lao (the Lao government is incredibly inconsistent in this respect, though they tend to follow the old French methods), we have created a transcription system similar to that used in Lonely Planet's *Thai phrasebook*, since the languages have a virtually identical sound system. The public and private sectors in Laos are gradually moving towards a more internationally recognisable system along the lines of the Royal Thai General Transcription (which is fairly readable across a large number of language types). This can also be problematic, however, as when an 'r' is used where an 'h' or 'l' is the actual sound, simply because the Lao symbols for these sounds look so much like the Thai 'r' (spoken Lao has no 'r' sound). Don't worry though, with our system, you'll be fine.

VOWELS

The x in the Lao script indicates the position that a consonant must fill to produce a written syllable.

xິ	i	as the 'i' in 'it'
xີ	ii	as the 'ee' in 'feet' or 'tea'
xະ, xັx	a	as the 'u' in 'fun'
xາ	aa	as the 'a' in 'father'
ແx	ae	as the 'a' in 'bat'
ເxະ, ເxັx	e	as the 'e' in 'hen'
ເx	eh	as the 'a' in 'hate'
xຸ	u	as the 'u' in 'flute'
xູ	uu	as the 'oo' in 'food'
xໍ, ອ	aw	as the 'aw' in 'jaw'
xຳ	am	as the 'um' in 'rum'
ເxິ, ເxີ	oe	as the 'uh' in 'huh'
xຶ, xື	eu	similar to the 'i' in 'sir' or the 'eux' in the French 'deux'
Diphthongs		
ໄx, ໃx	ai	as the 'i' in 'pipe'
ເxົາ, xາວ	ao	as the 'ow' in 'now'
ໂxະ, xົ	o	as the 'o' in 'phone'
ໂx	oh	as the 'o' in 'toe'
ເxືອ	eua	combine **eu** and **a**
ເxັຍ, ເxຍ, xຽx	ia	combine **i** and **a**, or the 'ie' in the French 'rien'
xົວ	ua	as the 'our' in 'tour'
xວຍ	uay	as the 'ewey' in 'Dewey'
xິວ	iu	as the 'ew' in 'yew'
xຽວ	iaw	similar to the 'io' in 'Rio'
ແxວ	aew	combine **ae** and **w**
ເxວ	ehw	combine **eh** and **w**
ເxັວ	ew	same as **ehw** above, but shorter
ເxີຍ	oei	combine **oe** and **i**
xອຍ	awy	combine **aw** and **y**

PRONUNCIATION

CONSONANTS

Some Lao consonant sounds may be represented by two separate characters, just as 'ph' and 'f' are pronounced the same way in English.

ສ, ຊ	s	as the 's' in 'soap'
ຝ, ຟ	f	same as the 'f' in 'fan'
ດ	d	as the 'd' in 'dodo'
ຕ	t	as the 't' in 'stop', similar to 'd'
ຖ, ທ	th	as the 't' as in 'tea'
ກ	k	as the 'k' in 'skin'
ຂ,ຄ	kh	as the 'k' in 'kite'
ບ	b	as the 'b' in 'boy'
ປ	p	as the 'p' in 'spin', similar to 'b'
ຜ, ພ	ph	as the 'p' in 'put' (but never as the 'ph' in 'phone')
ມ, ໝ	m	as the 'm' in 'man'
ນ, ໜ	n	as the 'n' in 'nun'
ງ	ng	as the 'ng' in 'sing'
ຍ	ny	similar to the 'ni' in 'onion'
ຈ	j	similar to the second 't' in 'stature'
ຢ	y	as the 'y' in 'yo-yo'
ລ, ຫຼ	l	as the 'l' in 'lick'
ວ	w	as the 'w' in 'wing'
ຫ, ຮ	h	as the 'h' in 'home'

PLAY IT AGAIN ...

ໆ	this character denotes repetition of the previous word

VARIATIONS IN TRANSLITERATIONS

In Laos you may come across many instances where the transliteration of vowels and consonants differs significantly, as in 'Louang' for Luang, 'Khouang' for Khuang or 'Xaignabouli' for Sainyabuli. The French spellings are particularly inconsistent in the use of the vowel 'ou', which in their transcriptions sometimes corresponds to a 'u' and sometimes to 'w'. An 'o' is often used for a short 'aw', as in 'Bo', which is pronounced more like baw.

Instances of 'v' in transcribed Lao words are generally pronounced more like a 'w'. For example, 'Vang Vieng' sounds more like Wang Wieng. In Vientiane, some of the older, educated upper class employ a strong 'v' rather than a 'w' sound.

Many standard place names in Roman script use an 'x' for what in English is 's'. There's no difference in pronunciation of the two; pronounce all instances of 'x' as 's'; for example, 'Xieng' should be pronounced sieng.

Finally, there's no 'r' sound in modern spoken Lao. When you see an 'r' in transcribed Lao, it's usually an old Lao or borrowed Thai transliteration; it should be pronounced like an 'l' in this case. Setthathirat (the name of a historic Lao king and common street name), for example, should actually be transcribed with an 'l' instead of an 'r' but usually isn't.

WIT & WISDOM

The wise man is a good listener.

khón sá-làat nyáwm pẹn khón hûu-ják fang

ຄົນສະຫລາດຍອມ ເປັນຄົນຮູ້ຈັກຟັງ

TONES

Traditionally, Lao is described as a monosyllabic, tonal language, like various forms of Thai and Chinese. Borrowed words from Sanskrit, Pali, French and English often have two or more syllables, however. Many syllables are differentiated by tone only. Consequently, the word sao, for example, can mean 'girl', 'morning', 'pillar' or 'twenty' depending on the tone. For people from non-tonal language backgrounds, this can take a bit of practice at first. Even when we 'know' the correct tone, our tendency to denote emotion, emphasis and questions through tone modulation often interferes with uttering the correct tone. So, the first rule in learning and using the tone system is to avoid overlaying your native intonation patterns onto Lao.

Vientiane Lao has six tones (compared with five in Standard Thai, four in Mandarin and up to nine in Cantonese). Three of the tones are level (low, mid and high) while three follow pitch inclines (rising, high falling and low falling). All six variations in pitch are relative to the speaker's natural vocal range, so that one person's low tone is not necessarily the same pitch as another person's. Hence, keen pitch recognition is not a prerequisite for learning a tonal language like Lao. A relative distinction between pitch contours is all that's necessary, just as it is with all languages (English and other European languages use intonation, too, just in a different way).

On a visual curve, the tones look like this:

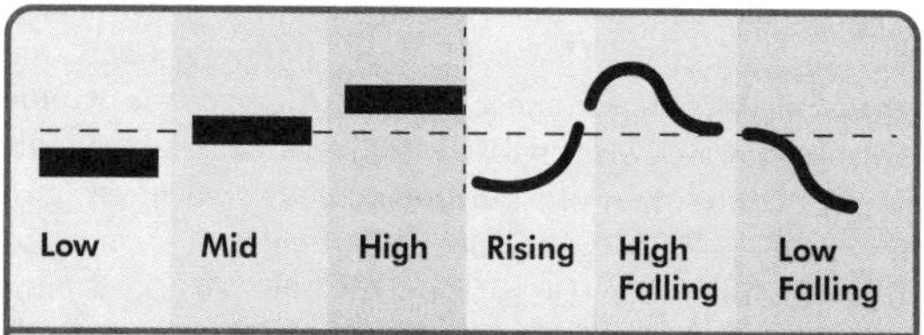

- The low tone is produced at the relative bottom of your conversational tonal range – usually flat and level (though not everyone pronounces it flat and level – some Vientiane natives add a slight rising tone to the end). For example, dii (ດີ, good).

- The mid tone is flat like the low tone, but spoken at the relative middle of the speaker's vocal range. No tone mark is used. For example, het (ເຮັດ, do).

- The high tone is flat again, this time at the relative top of your vocal range. For example, héua (ເຮືອ, boat).

- The rising tone begins a bit below the mid tone and rises to just at or above the high tone. For example, săam (ສາມ, three).

- The high falling tone begins at or above the high tone and falls to the mid level. For example, sâo (ເຊົ້າ, morning).

- The low falling tone begins at about the mid level and falls to the level of the low tone. For example, khào (ເຂົ້າ, rice).

SCRIPT

This section will help those interested in learning about the fascinating, if somewhat complicated, Lao writing system. Fear not – if you're eager to hit the streets and speak Lao, skipping this section will not hinder your ability to communicate.

Prior to the consolidation of various Lao méuang (principalities) in the 14th century, there was little demand for a written language. When a written language was deemed necessary by the Lan Xang monarchy, Lao scholars based their script on an early alphabet devised by the Thais (which in turn had been created by Khmer scholars who used Mon scripts as models!). The alphabet used in Laos is closer to the original prototype; the original Thai script was later extensively revised (which is why Lao appears 'older' to orthographists than Thai, even though it's newer as a written language).

Before 1975, at least four spelling systems were in use. As modern printing never really established itself in Laos (most advanced textbooks being in Thai, French or Vietnamese before the revolution), Lao spelling wasn't standardised until after the Pathet Lao takeover. The current system has been highly simplified by omitting all literally transcribed spellings from foreign loan words. Instead of transliterating the Sanskrit *nagara* (city) letter for letter, for example, the new script uses only the letters actually pronounced in Lao, na-kháwn. Every letter written is pronounced, which means Lao script can be learned much more quickly than Thai or Khmer, both of which typically attempt to transcribe foreign borrowings letter for letter no matter what the actual pronunciation is.

Other scripts still in use include láo thám (dhamma Lao), used for writing Pali scriptures, and various Thai tribal scripts, the most popular and widespread being that of the Thai Neua (which has become standardised via Xishuangbanna, China).

The Lao script today consists of 28 consonants (but only 20 separate sounds) and 35 vowel and diphthong possibilities (16 separate symbols in varying combinations). In addition to the consonant and vowel symbols are four tone marks, only two of which are commonly used to create the six different tones (in combination with all the other symbols).

Written Lao proceeds from left to right, though vowel-symbols may be written before, above, below, 'around' (before, above and after) or after consonants, depending on the sign. Although learning the alphabet is not difficult, the writing system itself is fairly complex, so unless you're planning a lengthy stay in Laos, it should perhaps be foregone in favour of learning to actually speak the language.

How Spelling Determines Lao Tones

Several features combine to encode the correct tone for each word or syllable in written Lao. To begin with, all Lao consonants are divided into three 'classes': high, mid and low, each of which follows its own set of tone rules. Once you've established which consonant class begins the syllable, you look for the absence or presence of a tone mark over the initial consonant. Modern written Lao has two tone marks: the mâi èhk (່) and the mâi thóh (້).

In standard Vientiane Lao, all syllables with a mâi èhk are spoken with the mid tone. Those with the mâi thóh are spoken with a low falling tone if they begin with a high-class consonant, or with a high falling tone if they begin with mid- or low-class consonants.

If there is no tone-mark over the syllable, then, in addition to knowing the consonant class, you must also take into consideration the length of the vowel and whether or not the word ends with that vowel or with a consonant. (This doesn't apply to tone-marked words, since they all end either with a vowel or with a nasal, ie, ng or n.)

Syllables with a stop final (p, t or k) combined with a long vowel take one set of tones (low falling for high- and mid-class consonants, high falling for low-class consonants), while those with short vowels take another (high tone for high- and mid-class consonants, mid tone for low-class consonants). In the case of short vowels without a final consonant, the tone is the same as for syllables with short vowels and stop finals.

For words of more than one syllable, each syllable has its own discrete tone, governed by the spelling of that syllable. Unlike Thai, there are no unwritten vowels in Lao, so the tone of one syllable never influences the following syllable – at least not in the written language.

The following charts show how these factors – consonant class, tone-mark, vowel length and syllable final – combine to encode the six tones in written Vientiane Lao. Although the system may seem rather complicated at first, once you've learned all the Lao characters, you can refer to these charts while learning to read and eventually internalise the Lao tone system.

Note that Lao dialects spoken in parts of Laos outside Vientiane Province follow their own tone rules. Also note that even the tone system for the Vientiane dialect is widely debated and true standardisation has yet to be achieved.

The Tonal System

Class	NTMNSF	mâi èhk	mâi thóh	SFLV	SFSV/SV
High	rising	mid	LF	LF	high
Mid	low	mid	HF	LF	high
Low	high	mid	HF	HF	mid

Examples with Transliteration

Class	NTMNS	mâi èhk	mâi thóh	SFLV	SFSV/SV
High	ຂາວ khăo	ຂ່າວ khao	ເຂົ້າ khào	ຫຼອດ lâwt	ສິດ sót
Mid	ດີ dii	ຕ່າງ taang	ເຈົ້າ jâo	ຈອກ jàwk	ເດັກ dék
Low	ເງິນ ngóen	ນັ່ງ nang	ແລ້ວ lâew	ເລືອດ lêuat	ທຸກ thuk

Key:

LF = low falling
HF = high falling
SFSV/SV = stop final, short vowel; or short vowel, no final consonant
SFLV = stop final, long vowel
NTMNS = no tone mark, no stop final

GRAMMAR

The following outline provides an introduction to the basics of Lao grammar – it is not a complete description, but it provides the tools to start building your own Lao sentences for those conversations that lead off the beaten track.

WORD ORDER

In general, word order in Lao is very significant. For example, dâi (ໄດ້) placed immediately before the verb marks past tense, while the same word appearing immediately after the verb means 'can'.

Although the basic word order in Lao sentences is subject-verb-object, it's not uncommon to place the object first, for emphasis.

I don't like that bowl.
thùay nân khàwy baw mak ຖ້ວຍນັ້ນຂ້ອຍບໍ່ມັກ
(lit: bowl that I no like)

NOUNS

Nouns never vary. They do not change to indicate plurality, and they do not need articles like 'a' or 'the'. Once you've learned the word for something, it stays the same. The word wat (ວັດ, temple), for example, never changes, no matter how many wat you're speaking about.

Verbs of physical action can be made into nouns by adding kąan (ການ) before the verb. Verbs describing abstract action – as well as adjectives – use khwáam (ຄວາມ) to form nouns.

to travel	dọen tháang	ເດີນທາງ
travel (n)	kąan dọen tháang	ການເດີນທາງ
to think	khit	ຄິດ
thought (n)	khwáam khit	ຄວາມຄິດ
good (adj)	dįi	ດີ
good (n)	khwáam dįi	ຄວາມດີ

ADJECTIVES

Lao adjectives always follow the nouns they modify, except in the names of certain food dishes (eg, 'grilled chicken' is pîng kai, ປີ້ງໄກ່) where the adjective precedes the noun. They don't change in any way to 'agree' with the noun.

In Lao, you don't need to insert the verb 'to be' when describing something. Instead of saying 'the house is red' as we do in English, the Lao comes out as simply 'house red'.

big house
héuan nyai ເຮືອນໃຫຍ່
(lit: house big)

delicious food
kheuang kín sâep ເຄື່ອງກິນແຊບ
(lit: food delicious)

The room is small.
hàwng nâwy ຫ້ອງນ້ອຍ
(lit: room small)

Comparatives

Basically any adjective in Lao can be used to make comparisons by adding kwaa (ກ່ວາ) to it.

good	dii	ດີ
better	dii-kwaa	ດີກ່ວາ
cheap	thèuk	ຖືກ
cheaper	thèuk-kwaa	ຖືກກ່ວາ

Superlatives

Any adjective may be made superlative by adding thii-sút (ທີ່ສຸດ).

delicious	sâep	ແຊບ
the most delicious	sâep thii-sút	ແຊບທີ່ສຸດ
big	nyai	ໃຫຍ່
biggest	nyai thii-sút	ໃຫຍ່ທີ່ສຸດ

Equivalence

To express equivalence or sameness, use khéu káp (ຄືກັບ, the same as) or khéu kạn (ຄືກັນ, the same).

That kind is the same as this kind.
sá-nit nân khéu káp sá-nit nîi ຊະນິດນັ້ນຄືກັບຊະນິດນີ້
(lit: kind that khéu káp kind this)

Lao customs are not the same.
pá-phéh-níi láo baw khéu kạn ປະເພນີລາວບໍ່ຄືກັນ
(lit: custom Lao no khéu kạn)

ADVERBS

Adjectives that can logically be used to modify action may function as adverbs in Lao. Usually this is indicated by doubling the adjective; this kind of adverb always follows the verb.

slow	sâa	ຊ້າ
slow horse	mâa sâa (lit: horse slow)	ມ້າຊ້າ
Drive slowly.	kháp lot sâa-sâa (lit: drive car slow-slow)	ຂັບລົດຊ້າໆ

Certain words and phrases function only as adverbs and, depending on the word or phrase, may either precede the verb or come at the end of the sentence.

Adverbs Before the Verb

ever	khóei	ເຄີຍ
never	baw khóei	ບໍ່ເຄີຍ
perhaps	bạang thíi	ບາງທີ
probably	àat já	ອາດຈະ
rarely	hǎa nyâak	ຫາຫຍາກ
sometimes	bạang theua	ບາງເທື່ອ
usually	pók-ká-tí	ປົກກະຕິ
yet; not yet	nyáng	ຍັງ

Adverbs at the End of a Sentence

also	khéu kạn	ຄືກັນ
always	lêuay lêuay	ເລື້ອຍໆ
immediately	thán thíi	ທັນທີ
often	lêuay	ເລື້ອຍ
only	thao-nân	ເທົ່ານັ້ນ

PRONOUNS

Demonstrative Pronouns

Demonstrative pronouns are the verbal equivalent of pointing.

Pronoun	with Noun	as a Question
this nîi ນີ້	this plate jạan nîi ຈານນີ້ (lit: plate nîi)	What's this? nîi maen nyăng ນີ້ແມ່ນຫຍັງ (lit: nîi be what)
that nân ນັ້ນ	that plate jạan nân ຈານນັ້ນ (lit: plate nân)	How much is that? nân thao-dại ນັ້ນເທົ່າໃດ (lit: nân equal what)
these lăo nîi ເຫຼົ່ານີ້	these plates jạan lăo nîi ຈານເຫຼົ່ານີ້ (lit: plate lăo nîi)	What are these? lăo nîi maen nyăng ເຫຼົ່ານີ້ແມ່ນຫຍັງ (lit: lăo nîi be what)
those lăo nân ເຫຼົ່ານັ້ນ	those plates jạan lăo nân ຈານເຫຼົ່ານັ້ນ (lit: plate lăo nân)	How much are those? lăo nân thao-dại ເຫຼົ່ານັ້ນເທົ່າໃດ (lit: lăo nân equal what)

Personal Pronouns

Lao has 10 common personal pronouns. They aren't used as frequently as their English equivalents since Lao is a 'subject-weak' language in which the subject of a sentence is often omitted after the first reference. There's no distinction between subject and object pronouns (ie, 'I' and 'me').

All Purpose Pronouns

The pronouns in this box will get you through your conversations, but as the opportunity arises, take the time to get to know some of the politer or more appropriate pronouns (some are given in the sections following) – they offer a little more insight into Lao culture.

I/me	khàwy	ຂ້ອຍ
he/she	khăo	ເຂົາ
it	mán	ມັນ
you (sg)	jâo	ເຈົ້າ
you (pl)	phûak jâo	ພວກເຈົ້າ
we	phûak háo	ພວກເຮົາ
us	phûak khàwy	ພວກຂ້ອຍ
they	phûak khăo	ພວກເຂົາ

First Person – I/We

I/me (to most people)
  khàwy ຂ້ອຍ
I/me (when speaking to elders or people with high status)
  kháa-nâwy ຂ້ານ້ອຍ
we/us
  phûak háo; phûak khàwy ພວກເຮົາ/ພວກຂ້ອຍ
  (lit: group we; group us)

Second Person – You

you (sg)	jâo	ເຈົ້າ
you (pl)	phûak jâo (lit: group you)	ພວກເຈົ້າ

The general all-purpose 'you' is jâo.

The pronoun thaan (ທ່ານ) is reserved for people in high social positions such as monks or government officials. You may also use it with Lao who are substantially older than you to show respect, although jâo is sufficient.

Other Terms of Address

Other terms of address you may hear, but probably won't use, include:

lúng	ລຸງ	to an older man (lit: uncle)
pâa	ປ້າ	to an older woman (lit: aunt)
tọh	ໂຕ	to a lover or other intimate relation
êuay	ເອື້ອຍ	to a female or social equal (lit: older sister)
âai	ອ້າຍ	to a male or social equal (lit: older brother)
nâwng	ນ້ອງ	to someone of any gender younger than you (lit: younger sibling)

None of these kinship terms is appropriate for use by a foreigner with an elementary command of Lao.

Third Person – He/She/It/They

he/she (when speaking of most people)
  khǎo — ເຂົາ

he/she (when speaking of elders or monks)
  phoen — ເພິ່ນ

he/she (when speaking about people you know)
  láo — ລາວ

he/she (when speaking about persons with high status)
  thaan — ທ່ານ

it (inanimate objects and animals)
  mán — ມັນ

they
  phûak added before khǎo, láo or phoen as with 'you' (plural) — ພວກ

In general, khǎo is the all-encompassing term; there is no gender or number distinction. When speaking of people you know personally, láo can be used, though for elders phoen is better. For monks phoen should be substituted (same as for second-person) to express respect. For example:

How many months has he been a monk?
  phoen bùat pẹn khúu-bạa dâi ják dẹuan lâew — ເພິ່ນບວດເປັນຄູບາໄດ້ຈັກເດືອນແລ້ວ
  (lit: phoen ordain be monk
    how many month already)

POSSESSION

Khǎwng (ຂອງ) is used to denote possession and is roughly equivalent to the preposition 'of' or the verb 'belongs to' in English.

my bag
thǒng khǎwng khàwy — ຖົງຂອງຂ້ອຍ
(lit: bag khǎwng I)

his/her seat
bawn nang khǎwng láo — ບ່ອນນັ່ງຂອງລາວ
(lit: place sit khǎwng he/she)

Does this belong to you?
nîi máen khǎwng jâo baw — ນີ້ແມ່ນຂອງເຈົ້າບໍ່
(lit: this be khǎwng you no)

The ever-versatile khǎwng can also be used as a noun to mean 'stuff' or 'things'.

She went to buy some things.
khǎo pai sêu kheuang khǎwng — ເຂົາໄປຊື້ເຄື່ອງຂອງ
(lit: she go buy some khǎwng)

For 'whose' use khǎwng phǎi (ຂອງໃຜ, belong who).

Whose plate is this?
jąan nîi maen khǎwng phǎi — ຈານນີ້ແມ່ນຂອງໃຜ
(lit: plate this be khǎwng phǎi)

VERBS

Tense

Lao verbs do not change their spellings or pronunciations to account for time references. Time is conveyed by context and by means of adding time indicators like 'today', 'tomorrow', 'yesterday', 'last year'and so on, or by adding markers that indicate ongoing action, completed action and to-be-completed action.

Out of context, without a time reference, the sentence **láo kįn kai** (ລາວກິນໄກ່) could mean 'She/He eats/ate/has eaten/will eat chicken'.

Adding **mêu-wáan-nîi** (ມື້ວານນີ້, yesterday) to the sentence, as in **mêu-wáan-nîi láo kįn kai** (ມື້ວານນີ້ລາວກິນໄກ່), gives this sentence a definite 'past' sense. Likewise **mêu-nîi** (ມື້ນີ້, today) **láo kįn kai** gives it a 'present' sense.

As in English, the time sense can be further qualified by the addition of words like 'often', 'seldom', 'every day', etc.

Ongoing Action

Verbs used in the absence of time markers such as 'yesterday' and 'tomorrow', are usually taken to indicate present or ongoing action.

They are playing guitar.
phûak khăo lìn kįi-tąa ພວກເຂົາຫລິ້ນກີຕາ
(lit: group he/she play guitar)

GRAMMAR

WIT AND WISDOM

If you are shy with the teacher you won't learn; if you are shy with women you won't get married.

ąai khúu baw dâi khwáam hûu ąai sûu baw dâi mía — ອາຍຄູບໍ່ໄດ້ຄວາມຮູ້ ອາຍຊູ້ບໍ່ໄດ້ເມຍ

Completed Action

The most common way of expressing completed action in Lao is by adding the past tense word lâew (ແລ້ວ) after the verb (if there is no direct or indirect object; after the object otherwise).

We went to Vientiane.
phûak khàwy pại wíeng jạn lâew — ພວກເຮົາໄປວຽງຈັນແລ້ວ
(lit: group I go Vientiane lâew)

I spent the money.
khàwy jai ngóen lâew — ຂ້ອຍຈ່າຍເງິນແລ້ວ
(lit: I spend money lâew)

Note that, as in the last example above, lâew can refer to a current condition that began in the immediate past.

Dâi (ໄດ້, to be able) also shows past tense but, unlike lâew, it's never used with present action. It immediately precedes the verb, and is often used in conjunction with lâew. It is more commonly employed in negative statements than in the affirmative.

Our friends didn't go to Luang Prabang.
pheuan phûak háo baw dâi pại lǔang pha-bạng — ເພື່ອນພວກເຮົາບໍ່ໄດ້ໄປຫລວງພະບາງ
(lit: friend group we no dâi go Luang Prabang)

To-Be-Completed Action

The future markers já (ຈະ) or sii (ຊິ) are used to mark an action to be completed in the future. It always appears directly before the verb.

She/He will buy rice.
láo já sêu khào — ລາວຈະຊື້ເຂົ້າ
(lit: she/he já buy rice)

Making Requests & Giving Commands

Khǎw (ຂໍ), a word that cannot be directly translated into English, is used to make polite requests. Depending on the context, it's roughly equivalent to 'please give me' or 'may I ask for'. Khǎw always comes at the beginning of a sentence, and is often used in conjunction with the added 'politener' dae (ແດ່) – spoken at the end of the sentence.

Please pass some rice.
: **khǎw khào dae** ຂໍເຂົ້າແດ່
: (lit: khǎw rice dae)

If you want someone to do something, you can politely preface the sentence with khǎw suay (ຂໍຊ່ວຍ, 'May I ask help?') or sóen (ເຊີນ, 'I invite you'). In English the closest equivalent is 'please'.

Please close the window.
: **khǎw suay pít pawng îam dae** ຂໍຊ່ວຍປິດປ່ອງອ້ຽມແດ່
: (lit: khǎw suay help close window dae)

Please sit down.
: **sóen nang** ເຊີນນັ່ງ
: (lit: sóen sit)

To express a greater sense of urgency, use dòe (ເດີ້) at the end of a sentence.

Close the door.
: **pít pá-tụu dòe** ປິດປະຕູເດີ້
: (lit: close door dòe)

TO BE

The verb 'to be' in Lao is much more limited in function than its English counterpart. There are two forms – **maen** (ແມ່ນ) and **pẹn** (ເປັນ) – which are only used to join nouns and/or pronouns. They are not used to join nouns or pronouns with adjectives (see Adjectives, page 24).

As a rule, use **maen** for objects and **pẹn** for people.

This is a pedicab.
ạn-nîi maen sǎam-lâw ອັນນີ້ແມ່ນສາມລໍ້
(lit: this **maen** pedicab)

I'm a musician.
khàwy pẹn nak-dọn-tịi ຂ້ອຍເປັນນັກດົນຕີ
(lit: I **pẹn** musician)

Pẹn is also used to show ability (see Can, page 38) and and can as well mean 'to have' when describing a person's condition (see To Have, page 35).

If you want to say 'there is ...' or 'there are ...', the verb **míi** (ມີ , 'to have') is used instead of **pẹn**. **Míi** here means 'to have' in the sense of 'to exist' – you're likely to hear it in sentences like:

In Vientiane, there are many cars.
yuu wiéng jạn míi lot lǎai ຢູ່ວຽງຈັນມີລົດຫລາຍ
(lit: stay Vientiane **míi** car many)

There's a large Buddha image at Wat Ong Teu.
wat ọng têu míi pha-phut-tha-hûup nyai ວັດອົງຕື້ມີ ພະພຸດທະຮູບໃຫຍ່
(lit: Wat Ong Teu **míi** Buddha-image big)

TO HAVE

Mı́i (ມີ) means 'to have' and, as mentioned on page 34, can also be used to mean 'there is' or 'there are'.

I have a bicycle.
khàwy mı́i lot thìip ຂ້ອຍມີລົດຖີບ
(lit: I **mı́i** vehicle pedal)
Do you have fried rice noodles?
mı́i phát fŏe baw ມີພັດເຝີບໍ່
(lit: **mı́i** fry rice-noodle no)

Pę̨n, 'to be', is used in the sense of 'to have' when describing a person's condition.

I have a fever.
khàwy pen khài ຂ້ອຍເປັນໄຂ້
(lit: I **pę̨n** fever)

She/He has a cold.
láo pę̨n wát ລາວເປັນຫວັດ
(lit: she/he **pę̨n** common-cold)

GRAMMAR DOESN'T RULE!

Grammar rules are certainly made to be broken – don't be afraid to experiment with some of the phrases and formulas you find in this section. Communicate in any way you can, string words together and don't hesitate to create a few 'interesting' sentences! The finer points will come ...

NEGATIVES

Baw (ບໍ່, no) is the main negative marker in Lao. Nyáng (ຍັງ) is also used to mean 'not yet' in answer to questions that end in lâew baw (ແລ້ວບໍ່, see Questions, page 39). Nyáng is placed before baw in a complete sentence, or alone to mean simply 'Not yet'.

Any verb or adjective may be negated by the insertion of baw immediately before it.

She/He isn't thirsty.
láo baw yàak nâm ລາວບໍ່ຢາກນ້ຳ
(lit: she/he baw want water)

I don't have any cash.
khàwy baw míi ngóen ຂ້ອຍບໍ່ມີເງິນ
(lit: I baw have money)

We're not French.
phûak háo baw pẹn khón fa-lang ວກເຮົາບໍ່ເປັນຄົນຝະລັ່ງ
(lit: group we baw be people French)

John has never gone to Savannaket.
john baw khóei pại sa-wăn-na-khèt ຈອນບໍ່ເຄີຍໄປ ສະຫວັນນະເຂດ
(lit: John baw ever go Savannaket)

We won't go to Pakse tomorrow.
mêu eun phûak háo baw pại pàak-séh ມື້ອື່ນພວກເຮົາ ບໍ່ໄປປາກເຊ
(lit: day other group we baw go Pakse)

You haven't eaten yet.
jâo nyáng baw thán kịn khào ເຈົ້າຍັງບໍ່ທັນກິນເຂົ້າ
(lit: you nyáng baw yet eat rice)

MODALS

Like most other languages, Lao makes use of words like 'should', 'want to', 'need to' or 'can' in conjunction with verbs to express obligation, want/need and ability (eg, must do, need to do, can do').

Obligation

Khúan (ຄວນ) serves as 'should' or 'ought to', usually in conjunction with jà, the marker for to-be-completed action.

You should eat.
jâo khúan já kịn khào — ເຈົ້າຄວນຈະກິນເຂົ້າ
(lit: you khúan já eat rice)

She/He shouldn't do that.
láo baw khúan hét naew nân — ລາວບໍ່ຄວນເຮັດແນວນັ້ນ
(lit: she/he no khúan do like that)

Want

Yàak (ຢາກ) is placed in front of the verb to express 'want' or 'desire'.

The dog wants to eat.
mǎa yàak kịn khào — ໝາຢາກກິນເຂົ້າ
(lit: dog yàak eat rice)

I don't want to walk.
khàwy baw yàak nyaang — ຂ້ອຍບໍ່ຢາກຍ່າງ
(lit: I no yàak walk)

When 'want' is used with a noun, it takes the form of either ạo (ເອົາ, take) or yàak dâi (ຢາກໄດ້, want to get).

I want bananas.
khàwy ạo kûay — ຂ້ອຍເອົາກ້ວຍ
(lit: I ạo banana)

Tom wants a shirt.
thawm yàak dâi sèua — ທອມຢາກໄດ້ເສື້ອ
(lit: Tom yàak dâi shirt)

Need

The word tâwng (ຕ້ອງ) comes before verbs to mean 'must' or 'need to'. When using 'need' plus a noun, use tâwng-kąan (ຕ້ອງການ).

I must go to the market.
  khàwy tâwng pąi tá-làat — ຂ້ອຍຕ້ອງໄປຕະຫລາດ
  (lit: I tâwng go market)

We need to look for a house.
  háo tâwng hǎa héuan — ເຮົາຕ້ອງຫາເຮືອນ
  (lit: we tâwng seek house)

You don't have to stay here.
  jâo baw tâwng phák yuu-nîi — ເຈົ້າບໍ່ຕ້ອງພັກຢູ່ນີ້
  (lit: you no tâwng stay here)

I need a bicycle.
  khàwy tâwng-kąan lot-thìip — ຂ້ອຍຕ້ອງການລົດຖີບ
  (lit: I tâwng-kąan bicycle)

Can

Lao has three ways of expressing 'can': dâi, pęn and sǎa-màat Dâi (ໄດ້) means 'to be able to' or 'to be allowed to' and is the more general equivalent of the English 'can'. It always follows the verb (and negative marker and object, if any).

Can you go?
  pąi dâi baw — ໄປໄດ້ບໍ່
  (lit: go dâi no)

I can't go.
  pąi baw dâi — ໄປບໍ່ໄດ້
  (lit: go no dâi)

I can't eat pork.
  kįn sîin mǔu baw dâi — ກິນຊີ້ນໝູບໍ່ໄດ້
  (lit: eat piece pig no dâi)

Pẹn (ເປັນ) may mean 'can' in the sense of 'to know how to'. Like dâi, it ends the verb phrase.

She/He knows how to play guitar.
láo lìn kịi-tạa pẹn — ລາວຫລິ້ນກີຕາເປັນ
(lit: she/he play guitar pẹn)

Sǎa-màat (ສາມາດ) is used as 'can' to express physical possibility or ability. Unlike dâi and pẹn, it's placed before the verb.

I can't lift that.
khàwy baw sǎa-màat nyok an-nân kèun — ຂ້ອຍບໍ່ສາມາດຍົກອັນນັ້ນຂຶ້ນ
(lit: I no sǎa-màat lift classifier-that up)

QUESTIONS

Lao has two ways of forming questions: use of a question word like 'who', 'how', 'what', etc or through the addition of a tag like 'isn't it?' or 'no?' to the end of the sentence.

Many English-speakers instinctively place an English question inflection to the end of a Lao question; try to avoid doing this as it will usually throw off the Lao tones.

GRAMMAR

Question Words

Note the placement of Lao question words in a sentence. Some come at the beginning of the question, others at the end.

What?	nyǎng	ຫຍັງ

What do you need?
jâo tawng-kạan nyǎng — ເຈົ້າຕ້ອງການຫຍັງ
(lit: you need nyǎng)

How?	náew-dại (lit: manner which)	ແນວໃດ

How do you do it?
hét náew-dại — ເຮັດແນວໃດ
(lit: do náew-dại)

Who?	phǎi	ໃຜ

Who's sitting there?
phǎi nang yuu hân — ໃຜນັ່ງຢູ່ຫັ້ນ
(lit: phǎi sit stay there)

When?	wéh-láa dại (lit: time which)	ເວລາໃດ

When will you go to Luang Prabang?
wéh-láa dại já pại lǔang pha-bạng — ເວລາໃດຈະໄປ ຫລວງພະບາງ
(lit: wéh-láa dại future-marker go Luang Prabang)

Why?	pẹn nyǎng (lit: be what)	ເປັນຫຍັງ

Why are you so quiet?
pẹn nyǎng jâo mit thâe — ເປັນຫຍັງເຈົ້າມິດແທ້
(lit: pẹn nyǎng you quiet real)

How much?	thâo dại (lit: equal what)	ເທົ່າໃດ

How much is this?
nîi thao dại — ນີ້ເທົ່າໃດ
(lit: this thâo dại)

Where?	yuu sǎi (lit: stay where)	ຢູ່ໃສ

Where's the bathroom?
hàwng nâam yuu sǎi — ຫ້ອງນ້ຳຢູ່ໃສ
(lit: room water yuu sǎi)

Which?	ạn dại (lit: classifier which)	ອັນໃດ

Which one do you like?
jâo mak ạn dại
(lit: you like ạn dại)
ເຈົ້າມັກອັນໃດ

Tags

Just like in English, a 'tag' comes at the end of a sentence and requests confirmation of what has been proposed in that same sentence.

isn't it?/is it?	baw	ບໍ່

The weather's hot, isn't it?
ạa-kàat hâwn baw
(lit: air hot baw)
ອາກາດຮ້ອນບໍ່

right?	maen baw	ແມ່ນບໍ່

You're a writer, right?
jâo pẹn nak-khían maen baw
(lit: you be student maen baw)
ເຈົ້າເປັນນັກຂຽນແມ່ນບໍ່

or not?	lěu baw	ຫລືບໍ່

Do you want to go out or not?
yàak pại lìn lěu baw
(lit: want go play lěu baw)
ຢາກໄປຫລິ້ນຫລືບໍ່

yet?	lâew baw	ແລ້ວບໍ່

Have you eaten yet?
jâo kịn khào lâew baw
(lit: you eat rice lâew baw)
ເຈົ້າກິນເຂົ້າແລ້ວບໍ່

eh?	lěu	ຫລື

ANSWERS

To answer questions in Lao, you merely repeat the verb, with or without the negative particle baw (ບໍ່). Informally, a negative particle will do for a negative reply.

Do you want to drink tea?	yàak kịn nâm sáa baw (lit: want eat water tea no)	ຢາກກິນນ້ຳຊາບໍ່
Yes.	yàak kịn (lit: want eat)	ຢາກກິນ
No.	baw yàak kin (lit: no want eat)	ບໍ່ຢາກກິນ
Are you well?	sá-bạai-dịi baw (lit: well no)	ສະບາຍດີບໍ່
Yes.	sá-bạai-dịi (lit: well)	ສະບາຍດີ
No.	baw sá-bạai (lit: no well)	ບໍ່ສະບາຍ
Have you eaten yet?	kịn khào lâew baw (lit: eat rice already no)	ກິນເຂົ້າແລ້ວບໍ່
Yes.	kịn lâew (lit: eat already)	ກິນແລ້ວ
No.	nyáng (lit: yet)	ຍັງ
You're a teacher, aren't you?	jâo pẹn khúu maen baw (lit: you be teacher be no)	ເຈົ້າເປັນຄູແມ່ນບໍ່
Yes.	maen (lit: be)	ແມ່ນ
No.	baw maen (lit: no be)	ບໍ່ແມ່ນ
Are you happy?	dịi-jại lěu baw (lit: happy or no)	ດີໃຈຫລືບໍ່
Yes.	dịi-jại (lit: happy)	ດີໃຈ
No.	baw (lit: no)	ບໍ່

CLASSIFIERS

Classifiers or counters are words which define the category that an item being counted belongs to. These are comparable to words like 'slice' and 'sheet' in English (as in 'two slices of bread' or 'three sheets of paper').

To state a quantity of something in Lao, you first name the thing you want, then the number and finally the classifier or counter of the item – so five oranges is màak-kîang hàa nuay (ໝາກກ້ຽງຫ້າໜ່ວຍ, orange five classifier). Every noun that's countable in Lao takes a classifier.

Common Classifiers

animals, furniture, clothing	tọh	ໂຕ
candles, books	hŭa	ຫົວ
Buddha images	ọng	ອົງ
buses, cars, bikes, vehicles	khán	ຄັນ
fruit, balls	nuay	ໜ່ວຍ
glasses (of water, tea, etc)	jàwk	ຈອກ
houses	lăng	ຫລັງ
letters, newspapers (flatsheets)	sá-báp	ສະບັບ
monks	hùup	ຮູບ
pairs of items (people, things)	khuu	ຄູ່
people	khón	ຄົນ
pills, seeds, small gems	kaen	ແກ່ນ
plates (food)	jạan	ຈານ
rolls (toilet paper, film)	mûan	ມ້ວນ
round hollow objects, leaves	bại	ໃບ
sets of things	sut	ຊຸດ
slices (cakes, cloth)	phaen	ແຜ່ນ
small objects, miscellaneous	tọh	ໂຕ

If you don't know (or forget) the appropriate classifier, tọh (ໂຕ) may be used for almost any small thing. Alternatively, the Lao sometimes repeat the noun rather than not use a classifier at all.

PREPOSITIONS

above	tháang thóeng	ທາງເທິງ
across from	khâam káp	ຂ້າມກັບ
adjacent to	yuu khàang káp	ຢູ່ຂ້າງກັບ
around	hâwp	ຮອບ
at	yuu	ຢູ່
behind	tháang lăng	ທາງຫລັງ
beside	tháang khàang	ທາງຂ້າງ
from	tae	ແຕ່
in (and inside)	nái	ໃນ
in front of	tháang nàa	ທາງໜ້າ
of	khăwng	ຂອງ
on	thóeng	ເທິງ
opposite	kọng kạn khâam káp	ກົງກັນຂ້າມກັບ
under	kàwng	ກ້ອງ
with	káp/nám	ກັບ/ນຳ

CONJUNCTIONS

and	lae	ແລະ
because	phaw waa	ເພາະວ່າ
but	tae waa	ແຕ່ວ່າ
or	lĕu waa	ຫລືວ່າ
since	tâng tae	ຕັ້ງແຕ່
so (therefore)	phaw sá-nân	ເພາະສະນັ້ນ
so that (in order to)	pheua	ເພື່ອ
then	lâew	ແລ້ວ
when	mêua/wéh-láa	ເມື່ອ/ເວລາ

ການພົບປະກັບ ປະຊາຊົນ MEETING PEOPLE

The all-purpose Lao greeting (and farewell) is sa-bąai-dįi (ສະບາຍດີ). It's often accompanied by a nop (ນົບ), the palms-together gesture of respect, or by a light handshake. If someone says sá-bąai-dįi to you, you should reply with the same phrase. A smile and sá-bąai-dįi goes a long way toward calming the initial trepidation that locals may feel upon seeing a foreigner, whether in the city or the countryside.

YOU SHOULD KNOW ໜ້າຈະຮູ້

How are you?	sá-bąai-dįi baw	ສະບາຍດີບໍ່
I'm fine.	sá-bąai-dįi	ສະບາຍດີ
Thank you.	khàwp jąi	ຂອບໃຈ
And you?	jâo dęh	ເຈົ້າເດ
Thank you very much.	khàwp jąi lăi lăi	ຂອບໃຈຫລາຍໆ
It's nothing. (never mind; don't bother)	baw pęn nyăng	ບໍ່ເປັນຫຍັງ
Excuse me.	khăw thôht	ຂໍໂທດ

IT'S ALL IN THE HANDS

Traditionally the Lao greet each other not with a handshake but with a prayer-like, palms-together gesture known as a nop (ນົບ). If someone nop-s you, you should nop back (unless nop-ed by a child). In Vientiane and large cities, a light version of the Western-style handshake is commonly offered to foreigners.

To beckon someone to come towards you, wave your hand with the palm down. This same gesture can be used to hail public transport along the side of the road.

A quick lifting of the eyebrows is often used to express affirmation or consent.

GREETINGS ການທັກທາຍ

As well as **sá-bąai-dįi**, other common greetings – especially when meeting someone on the road – are **pąi săi** (ໄປໃສ, 'Where are you going?') and **kįn khào lâew baw** (ກິນເຂົ້າແລ້ວບໍ່, 'Have you eaten yet?'). As with the English 'How are you?', the answer doesn't usually matter. If you're just out for a stroll, a common reply to **pąi săi** is **nyaang lín** (ຍ່າງຫລິ້ນ), which roughly translates into 'I'm just walking for fun'.

The greeting **kin kháo lâew baw** carries an implicit invitation to dine together (even for just a quick bowl of noodles), hence you choose the reply based on whether you'd like to spend time with the greeter. Answer **nyáng** (ຍັງ, 'Not yet') if you're willing to accept a possible meal invitation; answer **kin lâew** (ກິນແລ້ວ, 'I've eaten already'), if you'd rather be on your way.

GOODBYES ລາກ່ອນ

As mentioned, a simple **sá-bąai-dįi** can be used as a farewell, especially if both speakers are leaving at the same time.

If you are leaving and the person you're speaking to is staying behind, you can say **láa kawn** (ລາກ່ອນ, 'leaving first') or **pąi káwn** (ໄປກ່ອນ, 'going first'). If you're the one staying, you bid farewell by saying **sôhk dįi** (ໂຊກດີ, 'good luck').

Whether you're staying or going, it can also be appropriate to say **phop kąn mai** (ພົບກັນໃໝ່), meaning 'We'll meet again' (roughly equivalent to 'See you later').

FORMS OF ADDRESS ການຮຽກເອີ້ນ

The Lao generally address each other using their first names with a kinship term or other title preceding it. Other formal terms of address include **thaan** (ທ່ານ, Mr) and **náang** (ນາງ, Miss or Mrs). Friends often use nicknames or kinship terms like **âai/êuay** (elder brother/sister), **nâwng** (younger sibling) or **lúng/pâa** (uncle/aunt) depending on the age differential. Young children can be called **lăan** (nephew or niece).

The following list includes kinship terms commonly used as forms of address for non-family members, based on relative age difference from the speaker. For more kinship terms, see Family on page 52.

elder sister	êuay	ເອື້ອຍ
elder brother	âai	ອ້າຍ
younger sibling	nâwng	ນ້ອງ
grandmother	mae thào	ແມ່ເຖົ້າ
grandfather	phaw thào	ພໍ່ເຖົ້າ
aunt	pâa	ປ້າ
uncle	lúng	ລຸງ
niece/nephew	lǎan	ຫລານ

BODY LANGUAGE ພາສາໂບ້ຍ

Non-verbal behaviour is very important in Laos, perhaps more important than in most Western countries.

When walking indoors in front of someone who's sitting down, you should stoop a little as a sign of respect.

The feet are the lowest part of the body (spiritually as well as physically) so don't point your feet at people or point at things with your feet. In the same context, the head is regarded as the highest part of the body, so don't touch the Lao on the head either.

SIN-FUL

Wearing clothes that bare the thighs, shoulders or breasts is often perceived as improper or disrespectful behaviour in Laos. Long trousers and walking shorts for men and women, as well as skirts, are acceptable attire. Tank tops, sleeveless blouses and short skirts or shorts are not. Many visiting women find that the traditional Lao sìn, a long patterned skirt, makes fine travel wear. For Lao women, such dress is mandatory for visits to government offices and museums.

FIRST ENCOUNTERS ການປະເສີນໜ້າຄັ້ງທຳອິດ

What's your name?
  jâo seu nyăng — ເຈົ້າຊື່ຫຍັງ

My name is ...
  khàwy seu ... — ຂ້ອຍຊື່ ...

Glad to know you.
  nyín dịi thii dâi hûu-ják — ຍິນດີທີ່ໄດ້ຮູ້ຈັກ

MAKING CONVERSATION ການສົນທະນາ

We're friends.
  háo pẹn pheuan kạn — ເຮົາເປັນເພື່ອນກັນ

We're relatives.
  háo pẹn phii-nâwng kạn — ເຮົາເປັນພີ່ນ້ອງກັນ

I've come on business.
  khàwy máa het thu-la-kít — ຂ້ອຍມາເຮັດທຸລະກິດ

I've come on pleasure.
  khàwy máa thîaw — ຂ້ອຍມາທ່ຽວ

Nice weather, isn't it?
  aa-káat dịi maen baw — ອາກາດດີແມ່ນບໍ່

It's quite hot in Laos.
  meúang láo hâwn lăai — ເມືອງລາວຮ້ອນຫລາຍ

I like it here.
  khàwy mak yuu nîi — ຂ້ອຍມັກຢູ່ນີ້

May I have your address?
  khăw thii-yuu khăwng jâo dâi baw — ຂໍທີ່ຢູ່ຂອງເຈົ້າໄດ້ບໍ່

This is my address.
  nîi maen thii-yuu khăwng khàwy — ນີ້ແມ່ນທີ່ຢູ່ຂອງຂ້ອຍ

address	thii-yuu	ທີ່ຢູ່
fluent	lian lăai	ຫລ່ຽນໄຫລ
friend	pheuan	ເພື່ອນ
language	pháa-săa	ພາສາ
phone number	nám-bọe thóh-la-sáp	ນຳເບີ້ໂທລະສັບ
study/learn	hían	ຮຽນ

MEETING PEOPLE

BREAKING THE LANGUAGE BARRIER — ຄວາມຫຍຸ້ງຫຍາກດ້ານພາສາ

I can't speak (much) Lao.
khàwy pàak pháa-săa láo baw dâi (lăai) — ຂ້ອຍປາກພາສາລາວບໍ່ໄດ້(ຫລາຍ)

I can't speak Lao well.
khàwy pàak pháa-săa láo baw keng — ຂ້ອຍປາກພາສາລາວບໍ່ເກັ່ງ

Can you speak English?
jâo pàak pháa-săa ąng-kít dâi baw — ເຈົ້າປາກພາສາອັງກິດໄດ້ບໍ່

A little.
náwy neung — ໜ້ອຍໜຶ່ງ

I speak ... [insert country name from page 50]
khàwy pàak pháa-săa ... — ຂ້ອຍປາກພາສາ ...

Please speak slowly.
ká-lu-náa wâo sâa-sâa — ກະລຸນາເວົ້າຊ້າໆ

Please repeat.
ká-lu-náa wâo khéun mai — ກະລຸນາເວົ້າຄືນໃໝ່

Forgive me, I don't understand.
khăw thôht, khàwy baw khào jại — ຂໍໂທດຂ້ອຍບໍ່ເຂົ້າໃຈ

I/We don't understand.
baw khào jại — ບໍ່ເຂົ້າໃຈ

Do you understand?
jâo khào jại baw — ເຈົ້າເຂົ້າໃຈບໍ່

What?
nyăng — ຫຍັງ

What did you say?
jâo wâo nyăng — ເຈົ້າເວົ້າຫຍັງ

Can you teach me Lao?
jâo săwn pháa-săa láo hâi khàwy dâi baw — ເຈົ້າສອນພາສາລາວໃຫ້ຂ້ອຍໄດ້ບໍ່

What do you call this in Lao?
ạn-nîi pháa-săa láo waa nyăng — ອັນນີ້ພາສາລາວວ່າຫຍັງ

NATIONALITIES ສັນຊາດ

Where do you come from?	jâo máa tae sai	ເຈົ້າມາແຕ່ໃສ
I come from ...	khàwy máa tae ...	ຂ້ອຍມາແຕ່ ...
I'm from ...	khàwy pẹn khón ...	ຂ້ອຍເປັນຄົນ ...
Australia	ạw-sá-tạa-líi	ອົສຕາລີ
Canada	kạa-náa-dạa	ການາດາ
China	jịin	ຈີນ
Denmark	dạen-mâak	ແດນມາກ
England	ạng-kít	ອັງກິດ
Europe	yúu-lôhp	ຢູໂລບ
France	fa-lang	ຝະລັ່ງ
Germany	yóe-la-mán	ເຢຍລະມັນ
Holland	háwn-láen	ຮອລແລນ
India	in-dia	ອິນເດຍ
Italy	íi-tạa-lịi	ອີຕາລີ
Japan	nyii-pun	ຍີ່ປຸ່ນ
Laos	láo	ລາວ
New Zealand	níu síi-láen	ນິວຊີແລນ
Singapore	sǐng-a-pọh	ສິງກາໂປ
Spain	sá-pẹhn	ສະແປນ
Sweden	sá-wíi-dẹn	ສະວີດເດັນ
Switzerland	sá-wit-sóe-láen	ສະວິດເຊີແລນ
Taiwan	tâi-wǎn	ໄຕ້ຫວັນ
USA	ạa-méh-li-kạa	ອາເມລິກາ

WIT AND WISDOM

You don't need to teach an alligator how to swim.

yaa sạwn khàe láwy nâm ຢ່າສອນແຂ້ລອຍນ້ຳ

AGE ອາຍຸ

Asking someone's age is a common question in Laos. It's not considered rude to ask strangers their age.

How old are you?	jâo ąa-nyu ják pįi	ເຈົ້າອາຍຸຈັກປີ
I'm ... years old.	kháwy ąa-nyu ... pįi	ຂ້ອຍອາຍຸ ... ປີ
Very young!	num lǎai	ໜຸ່ມຫລາຍ
Very old!	tháo lǎai	ເຖົ້າຫລາຍ

OCCUPATIONS ອາຊີບ

I'm a/an ...	khàwy pęn ...	ຂ້ອຍເປັນ ...
artist	sǐ-la-pįn	ສິລະປິນ
businessperson	nak thu-la-kít	ນັກທຸລະກິດ
diplomat	nak kąan-thûut	ນັກການທູດ
doctor	thaan mǎw	ທ່ານໝໍ
engineer	wit-sáa-wa-kąwn	ວິຊາວະກອນ
farmer	sáo-náa	ຊາວນາ
journalist	nak khao	ນັກຂ່າວ
lawyer	tha-nái-khwáam	ທະນາຍຄວາມ
musician	nak dǫn-tįi	ນັກດົນຕີ
policeman	tąm lùat	ຕຳຫລວດ
secretary	léh-khǎa-nu-kąan	ເລຂານຸການ
student	nak séuk-sǎa	ນັກສຶກສາ
teacher	khúu	ຄູ
traveller/tourist	nak thawng thiaw	ນັກທ່ອງທ່ຽວ
volunteer	ąa-sǎa-sá-mak	ອາສາສະໝັກ
worker	kąm-ma-kąwn	ກຳມະກອນ
I'm in the military.	tha-hǎan	ທະຫານ
I'm unemployed.	waang ngáan	ຫວ້າງງານ

FAMILY ຄອບຄົວ

Laos is a very family-orientated society, so enquiries about one's family are quite common. If you're asked about marriage or children, it's better to respond with the Lao for 'not yet' rather than 'I/We don't want children' or 'I/We have no plans to get married'.

Lao has no specific word for 'cousin'; if you must refer to this relationship, preface the appropriate Lao word for aunt or uncle with **lûuk khǎwng ...** (ລູກຂອງ ..., 'child of ...').

How many in your family?
khâwp khúa jǎo míi ják khón ຄອບຄົວເຈົ້າມີຈັກຄົນ

I have ... in my family.
[for numbers, see page 161]
míi ... khón ມີ ... ຄົນ

Are you married (yet)?
taeng-ngáan lâew lěu baw ແຕ່ງງານແລ້ວຫລືບໍ່

Yes, I'm married.
taeng-ngáan lâew ແຕ່ງງານແລ້ວ

I'm not married yet.
nyáng baw taeng-ngáan ຍັງບໍ່ແຕ່ງງານ

I'm single.
pẹn sóht ເປັນໂສດ

Do you have any children (yet)?
míi lûuk lâew baw ມີລູກແລ້ວບໍ່

I have ... child/children.
míi lûuk ... khón lâew ມີລູກ ... ຄົນແລ້ວ

I don't have children yet.
nyáng baw míi lûuk ຍັງບໍ່ມີລູກ

Family Members ສະມາຊິກຄອບຄົວ

aunt (older sister of either parent)	pâa	ປ້າ
child/children	lûuk	ລູກ
daughter	lûuk săo	ລູກສາວ
family	khâwp khúa	ຄອບຄົວ
father	phaw	ພໍ່
father's side		
grandfather	púu	ປູ່
grandmother	yaa	ຍ່າ
aunt	ạa	ອາ
uncle	ao	ອາວ
husband	phŭa	ຜົວ
mother	mae	ແມ່
mother's side		
grandfather	phaw thào	ພໍ່ເຖົ້າ
grandmother	mae thào	ແມ່ເຖົ້າ
aunt	nâa	ນ້າ
uncle	nâa bao	ນ້າບ່າວ
niece/nephew	lăan	ຫລານ
older sister	êuay	ເອື້ອຍ
older brother	âai	ອ້າຍ
parents	phaw-mae	ພໍ່ແມ່
relatives	phii-nâwng	ພີ່ນ້ອງ
son	lûuk sáai	ລູກຊາຍ
uncle (older brother of either parent)	lúng	ລຸງ
wife	mía	ເມຍ
younger sister	nâwng săo	ນ້ອງສາວ
younger brother	nâwng sáai	ນ້ອງຊາຍ
younger sibling	náwng	ນ້ອງ

THE POWER BEHIND THE ELEPHANT

Lao women have substantial gender parity in the workforce, inheritance, land ownership and so on, often more so than in many Western countries. The bad news is that, although women generally fare well in these areas, their cultural standing is a bit further from parity. An oft-repeated Lao saying reminds us that men form the front legs of the elephant, women the hind legs.

Lao Buddhism commonly holds that women must be reborn as men before they can attain nirvana, though many *dhamma* teachers point out that this presumption isn't supported by the suttas (discourses of the Buddha) or by the commentaries. But nevertheless it is a widespread belief.

While many Lao taboos can be bent a little without creating a huge fuss, the following one cannot. Aboard transport such as trucks, buses or riverboats in Laos, women are expected to ride inside. Any attempt to ride on the roof will be immediately discouraged. When asked why women can't sit on the roof, the usual Lao answer is **phít sàat-sá-náa** – 'it's against the religion', which is to say it's against Lao custom. Partially this is old-fashioned chivalry – 'it's too dangerous on the roof' – but mainly it's due to a deep-seated superstition that women's bodies should not intentionally occupy a physical space above a man's for fear of damaging men's spiritual status. Men wearing sacred tattoos or amulets often express the fear that such an arrangement will ruin the protection that these symbols are supposed to convey! The superstition runs to how laundry is hung out to dry. Women's clothing – especially underwear – is not to be hung above men's clothing.

FEELINGS ການສະແດງຄວາມຮູ້ສຶກ

The Lao are much less apt to express their feelings or emotions to strangers than most Western nationalities. Use discretion – any display or expression of strong emotion means a potential loss of face for both speaker and listener.

I feel ...	khàwy hûu-séuk ...	ຂ້ອຍຮູ້ສຶກ ...
angry	jại hâai	ໃຈຮ້າຍ
excited	teun tên	ຕື່ນເຕັ້ນ
happy	dịi jại	ດີໃຈ
lonely	ngǎo	ເຫງົາ
nervous (anxious)	ká-wón ká-wáai	ກະວົນກະວາຍ
proud	phúum jại	ພູມໃຈ
sad	sâo sòhk	ເສົ້າໂສກ
satisfied	pháw jại	ພໍໃຈ
sleepy	nguang náwn	ງ້ວງນອນ
surprised	pá-láat jại	ປະຫລາດໃຈ
tired	meuay	ເໝື່ອຍ
upset	ạa-lóm sǐa	ອາລົມເສຍ
I'm bored.	beua	ເບື່ອ
This is fun!	muan dịi	ມ່ວນດີ

OPINIONS ການອອກຄຳເຫັນ

I feel that ...	khàwy hûu-séuk waa ...	ຂ້ອຍຮູ້ສຶກວ່າ ...
I think that ...	khàwy khit waa ...	ຂ້ອຍຄິດວ່າ ...
I agree.	khàwy hěn dịi	ຂ້ອຍເຫັນດີ
I disagree.	baw hěn dịi	ບໍ່ເຫັນດີ
In my opinion ...	khwáam khit khǎwng khàwy ...	ຄວາມຄິດຂອງຂ້ອຍ ...
As for me ...	sǎm-láp khàwy ...	ສຳລັບຂ້ອຍ ...
It's not important.	baw sǎm-khán	ບໍ່ສຳຄັນ

COMMON INTERESTS ຄວາມສົນໃຈທົ່ວໄປ

What do you do in your spare time?
náі wéh-láah wàang jâo het nyăng — ໃນເວລາຫວ້າງ ເຈົ້າເຮັດຫຍັງ

I like ...	khàwy mak ...	ຂ້ອຍມັກ ...
I don't like ...	khàwy baw mak ...	ຂ້ອຍບໍ່ມັກ ...
Do you like ...?	jâo mak ... baw	ເຈົ້າມັກ ... ບໍ່
art	sí-la-pá	ສິລະປະ
cooking	taeng kịn	ແຕ່ງກິນ
dancing	fâwn	ຟ້ອນ
film	năng leuang	ໜັງເລື່ອງ
going out	àwk pại tháang nâwk	ອອກໄປທາງນອກ
music	dọn-tịi	ດົນຕີ
photography	thaai hûup	ຖ່າຍຮູບ
playing games	lìn kẹhm	ຫລີ້ນເກມ
playing soccer	lìn bạan-té	ຫລີ້ນບານເຕະ
playing sport	lìn kí-láa	ຫລີ້ນກິລາ
reading books	aan pêum	ອ່ານປຶ້ມ
shopping	pại sêu kheuang	ໄປຊື້ເຄື່ອງ
the theatre	boeng la-kháwn	ເບິ່ງລະຄອນ
travelling	thawng thiaw	ທ່ອງທ່ຽວ
watching TV	boeng thóh-la-that	ເບິ່ງໂທລະທັດ
writing	khĭan	ຂຽນ

SPORT

ກິລາ

Do you like sport?
jâo mak lìn kí-láa baw — ເຈົ້າມັກຫລິ້ນກິລາບໍ່

I like playing sport.
mak lìn kí-láa — ມັກຫລິ້ນກິລາ

I prefer to watch rather than play sport.
mak boeng lăai kwaa lìn — ມັກເບິ່ງຫລາຍກ່ວາຫລິ້ນ

Do you play ...?
jâo lìn baw ... — ເຈົ້າຫລິ້ນບໍ່ ...

Would you like to play ...?
jâo yàak lìn ... baw — ເຈົ້າຢາກຫລິ້ນ ... ບໍ່

HEAD OVER HEELS

Ká-tâw (ກະຕໍ້), a contest in which a woven rattan – or sometimes plastic – ball approximately 12cm in diameter is kicked around, is almost as popular in Laos as it is in Thailand and Malaysia.

The traditional way to play ká-tâw is for players to stand in a circle (the size of the circle depends on the number of players) and simply try to keep the ball airborne by kicking it soccer-style. Points are scored for style, difficulty and variety of kicking manoeuvres.

A popular variation on ká-tâw – and the one used in local or international competitions – is played with a volleyball net, using all the same rules as in volleyball except that only the feet and head are permitted to touch the ball. It's amazing to see the players perform aerial pirouettes, spiking the ball over the net with their feet.

baseball	bẹhs-bạwn	ເບສບອນ
basketball	bạan bâwng	ບານບ້ວງ
boxing	tịi múay	ຕີມວຍ
diving	dạm nám	ດຳນ້ຳ
gymnastics	kịm-náa-sa-tík	ກິມມນາສຕິກ
hockey	tịi-khíi thóeng nâm kâwn	ຕີຄີເທິງນ້ຳກ້ອນ
keeping fit	hak-sǎa sú-khá-phâap	ຮັກສາສຸຂະພາບ
martial arts	kạan sok múay	ການຊົກມວຍ
rugby	lak-bịi	ລັກບີ
skiing	lìn sá-kịi	ຫລິ້ນສະກີ
soccer (football)	bạan-té	ບານເຕະ
swimming	láwy nâm	ລອຍນ້ຳ
takraw	ká-tâw	ກະຕໍ້
tennis	tẹn-nîit	ເຕັນນິສ

ການເດີນທາງ GETTING AROUND

FINDING YOUR WAY ການຊອກທິດທາງ

Street signs in cities and towns in Laos are mostly written in Lao script only, although signs at major intersections in Vientiane are also written in French. The French designations for street names vary (eg, route, rue and avenue), but the Lao script always reads **tha-nǒn** (ຖະໜົນ), which means the same as all the French and English variations. Therefore, when asking directions it's always best to avoid possible confusion and use the Lao word **tha-nǒn**.

Excuse me, can you help me?
khǎw thôht, suay khàwy dâi baw ຂໍໂທດ ຊ່ວຍຂ້ອຍໄດ້ບໍ່

Where's the ...?	... yùu sǎi	... ຢູ່ໃສ
bus station	sá-thǎa-níi lot pá-jạm tháang	ສະຖານີລົດ ປະຈຳທາງ
bus stop	bawn jàwt lot pá-jạm tháang	ບ່ອນຈອດລົດ ປະຈຳທາງ
taxi stand	bawn jàwt lot thaek-sîi	ບ່ອນຈອດລົດ ແທັກຊີ

Which ... is this?	bawn nîi maen ... nyǎng	ບ່ອນນີ້ແມ່ນ ... ຫຍັງ
avenue/street/road	tha-nǒn	ຖະໜົນ
city	méuang	ເມືອງ
province	khwǎeng	ແຂວງ
village	muu bâan	ໝູ່ບ້ານ

I want to go to ...	khàwy yàak pại ...	ຂ້ອຍຢາກໄປ ...
I'm looking for ...	khàwy sâwk hǎa ...	ຂ້ອຍຊອກຫາ ...

What time will the ... leave?	... já àwk ják móhng	... ຈະອອກຈັກໂມງ
aeroplane	héua bịn	ເຮືອບິນ
boat	héua	ເຮືອ
minivan	lot tûu	ລົດຕູ້

DIRECTIONS ທິດທາງ

Excuse me, I'm looking for ...
khăw thôht, khàwy sâwk hăa ... ຂໍໂທດ ຂ້ອຍຊອກຫາ ...

How many kilometres from here?
jàak nîi pại ják kí-lóh-maet ຈາກນີ້ໄປຈັກກິໂລແມັດ

Turn ...	lîaw ...	ລ້ຽວ ...
left	sâai	ຊ້າຍ
right	khwăa	ຂວາ
Go straight ahead.	pại seu-seu	ໄປຊື່ໆ
Turn around.	lîaw káp	ລ້ຽວກັບ
Turn back.	káp máa	ກັບມາ
How far?	kại thao dại	ໄກເທົ່າໃດ
(not) far	(baw) kại	(ບໍ່) ໄກ
(not) near	(baw) kâi	(ບໍ່) ບໍ່ໃກ້
north	thit nĕua	ທິດເໜືອ
south	thit tâi	ທິດໃຕ້
east	thit tạa-wén àwk	ທິດຕາເວັນອອກ
west	thit tạa-wén tók	ທິດຕາເວັນຕົກ

STREET TALK

Street addresses are rarely used in Laos outside of Vientiane. Even in the capital city, jumbo drivers may be unable to locate a specific street address, since the numbering of buildings – both residential and commercial – tends to follow the order of construction, not the position of a building on a street.

Tha-nŏn (ຖະໜົນ) is the general all-purpose Lao word meaning street, road, avenue and so on. A typical street address – where they exist – might be 69 Thanon Lan Xang. Outside of the central Chanthabuli méuang (ເມືອງ, roughly, 'district') of Vientiane, few streets in Laos have signs bearing the name of the street. When such signs do exist, they are usually in Lao script only.

The méuang of Vientiane are broken up into bâan (ບ້ານ), which are neighbourhoods or villages associated with local wats. Wattay International Airport, for example, is in Ban Wat Tai, a village in the southern part of Muang Sikhottabong centred around Wat Tai.

BUYING TICKETS ການຊື້ແລະການຈອງປີ້

I would like a ticket.
  khàwy yàak dâi pîi — ຂ້ອຍຢາກໄດ້ປີ້

I would like two tickets.
  khàwy yàak dâi pîi săwng bại — ຂ້ອຍຢາກໄດ້ປີ້ສອງໃບ

Are there any tickets to ...?
  mii pîi pại ... — ມີປີ້ໄປ ...

How much per place (seat, deck space, etc)?
  bawn-la thao dại — ບ່ອນລະເທົ່າໃດ

How many departures are there ...?	... míi ják thîaw	... ມີຈັກຖ້ຽວ
today	mêu nîi	ມື້ນີ້
tomorrow	mêu eun	ມື້ອື່ນ

We would like to reserve ... places.
phûak háo yàak jąwng bawn ... bawn — ພວກເຮົາຢາກ ຈອງບ່ອນ ... ບ່ອນ

I'd like to change my ticket.
khàwy yàak pian pîi — ຂ້ອຍຢາກປ່ຽນປີ້

I'd like a refund on my ticket.
khàwy yàak khéun pîi — ຂ້ອຍຢາກຄືນປີ້

I'm sorry, I've changed my mind.
khǎw thôht, khàwy pian jąi lâew — ຂໍໂທດ ຂ້ອຍປ່ຽນໃຈແລ້ວ

AIR ທາງອາກາດ

Lao Aviation handles all domestic flights in Laos. You can purchase domestic tickets and make reservations at airline offices or travel agencies in every city that has an airfield.

aeroplane	héua bįn; nyón	ເຮືອບິນ; ຍົນ
airlines	kąan-bįn	ການບິນ
airport	doen bįn	ເດີ່ນບິນ
departures/flights	thîaw bįn	ຖ້ຽວບິນ
Lao Aviation	kąan-bįn láo	ການບິນລາວ
plane tickets	pîi héua bįn; pîi nyón	ປີ້ເຮືອບິນ; ປີ້ຍົນ

Is there a flight to ...?
míi thîaw bįn pąi ... — ມີຖ້ຽວບິນໄປ ...

When's the next flight to ...?
wéh-láa dąi míi thîaw bįn taw pąi ... — ເວລາໃດມີຖ້ຽວບິນຕໍ່ໄປ ...

What time will the plane leave?
héua bįn si khèun ják móhng — ເຮືອບິນຊິຂຶ້ນຈັກໂມງ

How long does the flight take?
sâi wéh-láa bįn dǫn pąan dąi — ໃຊ້ເວລາບິນດົນປານໃດ

BUS ລົດເມ

Where roads are surfaced, buses are an inexpensive and very acceptable way to get from one point to another. Outside the Mekong River Valley, Soviet, Vietnamese or Japanese trucks are often converted into passenger carriers by adding two long benches in the back. These passenger trucks are called **tháek-síi** (ແທັກຊີ, taxis), or in some areas **sǎwng-thǎew** (ສອງແຖວ, songthaew), which means 'two rows', in reference to the benches in the back.

Where public bus service isn't available, the Lao often travel long road distances by arranging rides with trucks carrying cargo from one province to another.

bus station
sá-thǎa-níi lot pá-jạm tháang (khíu lot méh) ສະຖານີລົດປະຈຳທາງ (ຄິວລົດເມ)

Which bus goes to ...?
lot khán dại pai ... ລົດຄັນໃດໄປ ...

Does this bus go to ...?
lot khán nîi pai ... baw ລົດຄັນນີ້ໄປ ... ບໍ່

How many departures are there today/tomorrow?
mêu-nîi/mêu-eun míi ják thîaw ມື້ນີ້/ມື້ອື່ນ ມີຈັກຖ້ຽວ

What time will the bus leave?
lot já àwk ják móhng ລົດຈະອອກຈັກໂມງ

What time's the ... bus?	**lot ... àwk ják móhng**	ລົດ ... ອອກຈັກໂມງ
first	**khán thii neung**	ຄັນທີໜຶ່ງ
last	**khán sut-thâai**	ຄັນສຸດທ້າຍ
next	**khán taw pại**	ຄັນຕໍ່ໄປ

Could you tell me when we get to ...?
jâo suay bàwk khàwy dâi baw wéh-láa pại hâwt ... ເຈົ້າຊ່ວຍບອກຂ້ອຍໄດ້ບໍ່ ເວລາໄປຮອດ ...

I want to get off.
khàwy yàak lóng ຂ້ອຍຢາກລົງ

TAXI ແທັກຊ

Each of the country's three largest towns – Vientiane, Luang Prabang and Savannakhet – has a handful of car taxis that are used by foreign businesspeople and the occasional tourist. The only place you'll find these taxis is at the airports (arrival times only) and in front of the larger hotels. Taxis like these can be hired by the trip, by the hour or by the day.

taxi	**lot thâek-síi**	ລົດແທັກຊີ

SAMLORS & JUMBOS ສາມລໍ້ແລະຈໍາໂບ້

Once a mainstay of local transport throughout urban Laos, the bicycle samlor has all but disappeared. When you can find them, samlor fares cost about the same as motorcycle taxis but are generally used only for distances less than 2km or so.

Three-wheeled motorcycle taxis are common in large cities. This type of vehicle can be called **thâek-síi** (ແທັກຊີ, taxi) or **săam-lâw** (ສາມລໍ້, 'three-wheels'). The larger ones made in Thailand are called **jąm-bǫh** (ຈໍາໂບ້, 'jumbos') and can hold four to six passengers. In Vientiane they are also sometimes called **túk-túk** (ຕຸກໆ) as in Thailand, while in the south (Pakse, Savannakhet) they may be called 'Skylab' because of the perceived resemblance to a space capsule! They can go anywhere a regular taxi can go, but aren't usually hired for distances greater than 20km or so.

jumbo	**jąm-bǫh**	ຈໍາໂບ້
samlor (pedicab)	**săam-lâw**	ສາມລໍ້

How much to ...?	
pại ... thao dại	ໄປ ... ເທົ່າໃດ
Too expensive. How about ... kìp?	
pháeng phôht. ... kíp dâi baw	ແພງໂພດ ... ກີບໄດ້ບໍ່
Agreed. Let's go.	
tók-lóng. lâew pại	ຕົກລົງ ແລ້ວໄປ
Drive slowly please.	
ká-lu-náa kháp sâa-sâa dae	ກະລຸນາຂັບຊ້າໆແດ່
Continue!	
kháp taw pại iik	ຂັບຕໍ່ໄປອີກ
Take the next street to the left/right.	
hâwt tháang taw pại lâew lîaw sâai/khwǎa	ຮອດທາງຕໍ່ໄປແລ້ວ ລ້ຽວຊ້າຍ/ຂວາ
Please wait here.	
ká-lu-náa thàa yuu nîi	ກະລຸນາຖ້າຢູ່ນີ້
Stop at the corner.	
ká-lu-náa jàwt yuu múum nîi	ກະລຸນາຈອດຢູ່ມູມນີ້
Stop here.	
jàwt yuu nîi	ຈອດຢູ່ນີ້

OUT FOR A TEN COUNT

1	neung	ໜຶ່ງ
2	sǎwng	ສອງ
3	sǎam	ສາມ
4	sii	ສີ່
5	hàa	ຫ້າ
6	hók	ຫົກ
7	jét	ເຈັດ
8	pàet	ແປດ
9	kâo	ເກົ້າ
10	síp	ສິບ

BOAT ເຮືອ

Rivers are the traditional highways and byways of Laos, the main thoroughfares being the Mekong, Nam Ou, Nam Khan, Nam Tha, Nam Ngum and Se Don. The Mekong is the longest and most important water route and is navigable year-round between Luang Prabang in the north and Don Khong in the south.

For long distances, large diesel river ferries with overnight accommodation are used. For shorter river trips (eg, from Luang Prabang to the Pak Ou caves), it's usually best to hire a river taxi, since the large river ferries only ply their routes a couple of times a week. The longtail boats, with engines gimbal-mounted on the stern, are the most typical, though for a really short trip, such as crossing a river, a rowboat can be hired.

Along the upper Mekong River between Luang Prabang and Huay Sai, Thai-built speedboats – shallow, five-metre-long skiffs with 40-hp outboard engines – are common.

boat	**héua**	ເຮືອ
boat taxi	**héua jâang**	ເຮືອຈ້າງ
cross-river ferry	**héua khàam fâak;**	ເຮືອຂ້າມຟາກ/
	héua bák	ເຮືອບັກ
longtail boat	**héua hăang nyáo**	ເຮືອຫາງຍາວ
row boat	**héua phái**	ເຮືອພາຍ
speed boat	**héua wái**	ເຮືອໄວ

Where do we get on the boat?
lóng héua yuu săi ລົງເຮືອຢູ່ໃສ
What time does the boat leave?
héua já àwk ják móhng ເຮືອຈະອອກຈັກໂມງ
What time does the boat arrive?
héua já máa hâwt ják móhng ເຮືອຈະມາຮອດຈັກໂມງ

USEFUL WORDS & PHRASES
ຄຳສັບແລະປະໂຫຍກທີ່ເປັນປະໂຫຍດ

arrive	máa hâwt	ມາຮອດ
bridge	khŭa	ຂົວ
charter vehicle	lot jâang	ລົດຈ້າງ
daily	pá-jạm mêu (thuk mêu)	ປະຈຳມື້ (ທຸກມື້)
detour	tháang wêhn	ທາງເວັ້ນ
drive	kháp	ຂັບ
early	sâo	ເຊົ້າ
fast	wái	ໄວ
hire/charter	jâang	ຈ້າງ
leave	àwk	ອອກ
pier	thaa héua	ທ່າເຮືອ
'regular vehicle' (ie, not a charter vehicle)	lot pá-jạm	ລົດປະຈຳ
seat	bawn nang	ບ່ອນນັ່ງ
slow	sâa	ຊ້າ
stop/park	jàwt	ຈອດ

What time does it leave here?
 já àwk jàak nîi ják móhng — ຈະອອກຈາກນີ້ຈັກໂມງ

What time does it arrive there?
 já pại hâwt phûn ják móhng — ຈະໄປຮອດພຸ້ນຈັກໂມງ

What time does the first vehicle leave?
 khán thii neung já àwk ják móhng — ຄັນທີ່ໜຶ່ງຈະອອກຈັກໂມງ

What time does the last vehicle leave?
 khán sút-thâai já àwk ják móhng — ຄັນສຸດທ້າຍຈະອອກຈັກໂມງ

What's the fare?
khaa dọen tháang thao dại ຄ່າເດີນທາງເທົ່າໃດ

How much per person?
khón-la thao dại ຄົນລະເທົ່າໃດ

I/We don't want to charter a vehicle.
baw yàak jâang lot ບໍ່ຢາກຈ້າງລົດ

I/We want to charter a vehicle.
yàak jâang lot ຢາກຈ້າງລົດ

Can you lower the price?
lut láa-kháa dâi baw ລຸດລາຄາໄດ້ບໍ່

Can you lower (the price) more?
lut ìik dâi baw ລຸດອີກໄດ້ບໍ່

Where does the vehicle depart from?
lot àwk yuu sǎi ລົດອອກຢູ່ໃສ

Where can we get on the vehicle?
khèun lot yuu sǎi ຂຶ້ນລົດຢູ່ໃສ

Is there anyone sitting here?
mii phǎi nang yuu nîi baw ມີໃຜນັ່ງຢູ່ນີ້ບໍ່

May I sit here?
nang bawn nîi dâi baw ນັ່ງບ່ອນນີ້ໄດ້ບໍ່

Can I put my bag here?
wáang thǒng yuu nîi dâi baw ວາງຖົງຢູ່ນີ້ໄດ້ບໍ່

Can you wait for me?
thàa khàwy dâi baw ຖ້າຂ້ອຍໄດ້ບໍ່

Can you wait here?
  jâo thàa yuu nîi dâi baw — ເຈົ້າຖ້າຢູ່ນີ້ໄດ້ບໍ່

Where are you going?
  pąi săi — ໄປໃສ

I want to go to ...
  khàwy yàak pąi ... — ຂ້ອຍຢາກໄປ ...

I'll get out here.
  khàwy si long bawn nîi — ຂ້ອຍຊິລົງບ່ອນນີ້

Which vehicle goes to ...?
  lot khan dąi pąi ... — ລົດຄັນໃດໄປ ...

When we arrive in ..., please tell me.
  wéh-láa hâwt ... — ເວລາຮອດ ...
  bàwk khàwy dae — ບອກຂ້ອຍແດ່

Can we stop over in ...?
  long phak yuu ... dâi baw — ລົງພັກຢູ່ ... ໄດ້ບໍ່

Stop here.
  jàwt bawn nîi — ຈອດບ່ອນນີ້

RENTING VEHICLES — ການເຊົ່າລົດ, ລົດຈັກແລະລົດຖີບ

Cars, motorcycles and bicycles can be rented in Vientiane and to a lesser degree in Luang Prabang. Bicycles can usually be arranged in smaller towns and are a good way of getting around since traffic is relatively light.

I'd like to rent a ...	khàwy yàak sao ...	ຂ້ອຍຢາກເຊົ່າ ...
bicycle	lot thìip	ລົດຖີບ
car	lot ọh-tọh	ລົດໂອໂຕ
motorcycle	lot ják	ລົດຈັກ
truck	lot bạn-thuk	ລົດບັນທຸກ

How much per/for ...?	... thao dại	... เท่าใด
hour	sua-móhng-la	ຊົ່ວໂມງລະ
day	mêu-la	ມື້ລະ
week	ạa-thit-la	ອາທິດລະ
month	dẹuan-la	ເດືອນລະ
three days	săam mêu	ສາມມື້

Does the price include insurance?
láa-kháa huam nám pá-kạn phái baw — ລາຄາຮ່ວມນຳປະກັນໄພບໍ່

Where's the next petrol station?
pâm nâm-mán taw pại yuu săi — ປ້ຳນ້ຳມັນຕໍ່ໄປຢູ່ໃສ

WAVING THE FLAG

Laos' national seal, often applied to official government publications, features a near-complete circle formed by curving rice stalks which enclose six component symbols of the productive proletarian state: Vientiane's Pha That Luang (representing religion); a checkerboard of rice fields (agriculture); gear cogs (industry); a dam (energy); a highway (transport); and a grove of trees (forestry). A label in Lao script at the bottom of the seal reads 'Lao People's Democratic Republic'.

The national flag consists of two horizontal bars of red (symbolising courage and heroism), above and below a bar of blue (nationhood) on which is centred a blank white sphere (the light of communism), sometimes also interpreted as a moon. This flag is flown in front of all government offices and by some private citizens on National Day (2 December). On this holiday the Lao national flag may be joined by a second flag featuring a yellow hammer and sickle centred on a field of red, the international symbol of communism.

Please fill the tank.
    ká-lu-náa sai nâm-man
    hài tem thăng
ກະລຸນາໃສ່
ນ້ຳມັນໃຫ້ເຕັມຖັງ

I'd like ... litres.
    sai ... lit
ໃສ່ ... ລິດ

Does this road lead to ...?
    tháang nîi pại hâwt ... baw
ທາງນີ້ໄປຮອດ ... ບໍ່

Please check the ...	ká-lu-náa kùat ...	ກະລຸນາກວດ ...
air	lóm	ລົມ
oil	nâm-mán	ນ້ຳມັນ
water	nâm	ນ້ຳ
tyre pressure	khwáam dạn khăwng yáang lot	ຄວາມດັນ ຂອງຢາງລົດ

CAR PROBLEMS ບັນຫາລົດ

We need a mechanic.
    phûak háo tâwng-kạan
    saang pạeng ják
ພວກເຮົາຕ້ອງການ
ຊ່າງແປງຈັກ

What make is it?
    yii hàw nyăng
ຍີ່ຫໍ້ຫຍັງ

Can you repair it?
    jâo pạeng dâi baw
ເຈົ້າແປງໄດ້ບໍ່

The battery's flat.
    màw fái awn
ໝໍ້ໄຟອ່ອນ

I have a flat tyre.
    yáang lot khàwy hua
ຢາງລົດຂ້ອຍຮົ່ວ

It's overheating.
    mán hâwn lăai phôht
ມັນຮ້ອນຫລາຍໂພດ

The radiator's leaking.
    màw nâm hua
ໝໍ້ນ້ຳຮົ່ວ

It's not working.
    mán baw het wîak
ມັນບໍ່ເຮັດວຽກ

Useful Words — ສັບທີ່ເປັນປະໂຫຍດ

battery	màw fái	ໝໍ້ໄຟ
brakes	hàam	ຫ້າມ
clutch	khâat	ຄາດ
drivers licence	bại á-nu-nyâat kháp khii	ໃບອະນຸຍາດຂັບຂີ່
engine	kheuang ják	ເຄື່ອງຈັກ
garage	uu sàwm pạeng lot	ອູ່ສ້ອມແປງລົດ
headlight	fái tạa tháang nàa	ໄຟຕາທາງໜ້າ
insurance	pá-kạn phái	ປະກັນໄພ
lights	fái	ໄຟ
mechanic	saang pạeng ják	ຊ່າງແປງຈັກ
motor oil	nâm-mán kheuang	ນ້ຳມັນເຄື່ອງ
oil	nâm-mán	ນ້ຳມັນ
petrol (gasoline)	nâm-mán (áet-sáng)	ນ້ຳມັນ (ແອັດຊັງ)
petrol station	pâm nâm-mán	ປ້ຳນ້ຳມັນ
puncture	hua/jáw	ຮົ່ວ/ເຈາະ
radiator	màw nâm	ໝໍ້ນ້ຳ
tyre	yạang lot	ຢາງລົດ
wheel	lâw	ລໍ້
windscreen	waen nàa	ແຫວ່ນໜ້າ

ສະຖານທີ່ພັກແຮມ ACCOMMODATION

In Laos, generally speaking, a 'single' means a room with one large bed that will sleep two, while a 'double' has two large beds. Room rates are thus quoted according to the number of beds a room has, rather than the number of guests who will be using the room. This is especially true for guesthouses. On the other hand, a few larger, Western-style hotels do calculate room tariffs according to the number of guests per room.

An 'ordinary room' (ຫ້ອງທຳມະດາ, hàwng thám-ma-dąa) usually means a less expensive room with a fan rather than with air-conditioning.

If you find yourself in a town or village where no hotels or guesthouses are available, or where they are all full, you may be invited to stay with local residents. In such cases you may be asked for a small fee. If not, it's good form to offer a gift – preferably food or something needed in the household – to your hosts.

FINDING ACCOMMODATION — ການຊອກສະຖານທີ່ພັກແຮມ

hotel	hóhng háem	ໂຮງແຮມ
guesthouse	héuan phak	ເຮືອນພັກ

Excuse me, is there a hotel nearby?
khǎw thôht, mįi hóhng háem yuu kâi nîi baw — ຂໍໂທດ ມີໂຮງແຮມຢູ່ໃກ້ນີ້ບໍ່

Is this a hotel?
nîi maen hóhng háem baw — ນີ້ແມ່ນໂຮງແຮມບໍ່

Is this a guesthouse?
nîi maen héuan phak baw — ນີ້ແມ່ນເຮືອນພັກບໍ່

Is there a place to stay here?
yuu nîi míi bawn phak baw — ຢູ່ນີ້ມີບ່ອນພັກບໍ່

We need a place to stay.
 phûak háo tâwng-kạan bawn phak — ພວກເຮົາຕ້ອງການບ່ອນພັກ

Can I/we stay here?
 phak yuu nîi dâi baw — ພັກຢູ່ນີ້ໄດ້ບໍ່

Can I/we sleep here?
 náwn yuu nîi dâi baw — ນອນຢູ່ນີ້ໄດ້ບໍ່

CHECKING IN — ການແຈ້ງເຂົ້າ

air-conditioning	ạe yẹn	ແອເຢັນ
bathroom	hàwng nâm	ຫ້ອງນ້ຳ
double room	hàwng náwn tịang khuu	ຫ້ອງນອນຕຽງຄູ່
fan	phat lóm	ພັດລົມ
hot water	nâm hâwn	ນ້ຳຮ້ອນ
not vacant	baw waang	ບໍ່ຫວ້າງ
room	hàwng	ຫ້ອງ
single room	hàwng náwn tịang diaw	ຫ້ອງນອນຕຽງດ່ຽວ
toilet	sùam	ສ້ວມ
vacant	waang	ຫວ້າງ

Do you have a room?
 míi hàwng baw — ມີຫ້ອງບໍ່

How many people?
 ják khón — ຈັກຄົນ

one person	neung khón; khón diaw	ໜຶ່ງຄົນ; ຄົນດຽວ
two people	sǎwng khón	ສອງຄົນ

How much per/for ...?	... thao dąi	... ເທົ່າໃດ
night	khéun-la	ຄືນລະ
week	ąa-thit-la	ອາທິດລະ
month	dèuan-la	ເດືອນລະ
three nights	săam khéun	ສາມຄືນ

It's too expensive.
pháeng phôht — ແພງໂພດ

I/We will stay two nights.
síi phak săwng khéun — ຊິພັກສອງຄືນ

Can you lower the price?
lut láa-kháa dâi baw — ລຸດລາຄາໄດ້ບໍ່

Can I/we look at the room?
khaw boeng hàwng dâi baw — ຂໍເບິ່ງຫ້ອງໄດ້ບໍ່

Do you have any other rooms?
míi hàwng eun íik baw — ມີຫ້ອງອື່ນອີກບໍ່

I/We want an ordinary room.
ąo hàwng thám-ma-dąa — ເອົາຫ້ອງທຳມະດາ

We need a ... room than this.	phûak háo tâwng-kąan hàwng ... nîi	ພວກເຮົາ ຕ້ອງການຫ້ອງ ... ນີ້
cheaper	théuk-kwaa	ຖືກກວ່າ
larger	nyai-kwaa	ໃຫຍ່ກວ່າ
smaller	nâwy-kwaa	ນ້ອຍກວ່າ
quieter	mit-kwaa	ມິດກວ່າ

WIT & WISDOM

It's easy to earn money but difficult to find kindness.

ngóen khám hăa dâi,
nâm jąi hăa yàak

ເງິນຄຳຫາໄດ້
ນ້ຳໃຈຫາຫຍາກ

REQUESTS & COMPLAINTS — ການຮ້ອງຂໍ ແລະຕໍ່ວ່າ

Is there ...?	míi ... baw	ມີ ... ບໍ່
a telephone	thóh-la-sáp	ໂທລະສັບ
hot water	nâm hâwn	ນ້ຳຮ້ອນ
I/We need (a) ...	tâwng-kạan ...	ຕ້ອງການ ...
another bed	tịang ìik	ຕຽງອີກ
blanket	phàa hom	ຜ້າຫົ່ມ
key	ká-jạe	ກະແຈ
pillow	mǎwn	ໝອນ
sheet	phàa pụu bawn	ຜ້າປູບ່ອນ
soap	sá-bụu	ສະບູ
towel	phàa set tọh	ຜ້າເສັດໂຕ

Can you clean the room?
á-náa-mái hàwng hài dae dâi baw — ອະນາໄມຫ້ອງໃຫ້ແດ່ໄດ້ບໍ່

This room isn't clean.
hàwng nîi baw sá-àat — ຫ້ອງນີ້ບໍ່ສະອາດ

There's no hot water.
baw míi nâm hâwn — ບໍ່ມີນ້ຳຮ້ອນ

Can you repair it?
jâo pạeng hài dae dâi baw — ເຈົ້າແປງໃຫ້ແດ່ໄດ້ບໍ່

CHECKING OUT — ການແຈ້ງອອກ

bill	bại bịn	ໃບບິນ
receipt	bai hap ngóen	ໃບຮັບເງິນ
service charge	khaa bạw-li-kạan	ຄ່າບໍລິການ
tax	pháa-sǐi	ພາສີ

I/We will return in two weeks.
ìik sǎwng ạa-thit síi káp máa — ອີກສອງອາທິດຊິກັບມາ

Can I store my bags here?
fàak kheuang yuu nîi dâi baw — ຝາກເຄື່ອງຢູ່ນີ້ໄດ້ບໍ່

LAUNDRY ຊັກເຄື່ອງ

Can you wash these clothes?
  sak séua phàa nîi dâi baw — ຊັກເສື້ອຜ້ານີ້ໄດ້ບໍ່

Where can I wash my clothes (myself)?
  khàwy sak séua phàa ẹhng dâi yuu sǎi — ຂ້ອຍຊັກເສື້ອຜ້າເອງໄດ້ຢູ່ໃສ

Is there a laundry near here?
  yuu thǎew nîi míi bawn sak lîit baw — ຢູ່ແຖວນີ້ມີບ່ອນຊັກລີດບໍ່

No starch.
  baw lóng pâeng — ບໍ່ລົງແປ້ງ

Add starch.
  lóng pâeng — ລົງແປ້ງ

These clothes aren't very clean.
  séua phàa nîi baw sá-áat thao dại — ເສື້ອຜ້ານີ້ບໍ່ສະອາດເທົ່າໃດ

Please wash them again.
  ká-lu-náa sak íik theua — ກະລຸນາຊັກອີກເທື່ອ

dry-clean	sak háeng	ຊັກແຫ້ງ
iron (n)	tạo lîit	ເຕົາລີດ
to iron	lîit	ລີດ
laundry service	bạw-li-kạan sak lîit	ບໍລິການຊັກລີດ

YES, NO, MAYBE...

'Yes' and 'No' don't exist in Lao in the same way as in English – it depends on the verb used in the question. Refer to page 42 for the basics on answering questions.

Useful Words — ຄຳສັບທີ່ເປັນປະໂຫຍດ

accommodation	bawn phak	ບ່ອນພັກ
to bathe	áap nâm	ອາບນ້ຳ
bathroom	tįang náwn	ຕຽງນອນ
bedroom	hàwng náwn	ຫ້ອງນອນ
breakfast	ąa-hăan sâo	ອາຫານເຊົ້າ
electricity	fái fâa	ໄຟຟ້າ
elevator (lift)	lip	ລິບ
entrance	tháang khào	ທາງເຂົ້າ
exit	tháang àwk	ທາງອອກ
fan	phat lóm	ພັດລົມ
food	ąa-hăan	ອາຫານ
lights	fái	ໄຟ

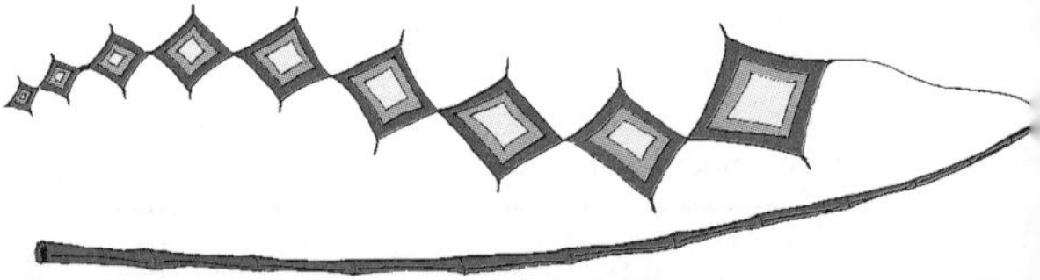

AROUND TOWN

LOOKING FOR ... ກຳລັງຊອກຫາ ...

Where is the ...?	... yùu sǎi	... ຢູ່ໃສ
How far is the ...?	... kại thao dại	... ໄກເທົ່າໃດ
I'm looking for the ...	khàwy sâwk hǎa ...	ຂ້ອຍຊອກຫາ ...
art gallery	háan wáang sá-dạeng sǐ-la-pá	ຮ້ານວາງສະແດງ ສິລະປະ
barber shop	hâan tát phǒm	ຮ້ານຕັດຜົມ
Buddhist temple; monastery	wat	ວັດ
cemetery	paa sâa	ປ່າຊ້າ
church	bòht khlit	ໂບດຄລິດ
city centre	kạang méuang	ກາງເມືອງ
... consulate	... kọng-sǔun	... ກົງສູນ
... embassy	... sa-thǎan-thûut	... ສະຖານທູດ
factory	hóhng ngáan	ໂຮງງານ
hotel	hóhng háem	ໂຮງແຮມ
market	ta-làat	ຕະຫລາດ
monument	á-nu-sǎa-wa-líi	ອານຸສາວະລີ
museum	phi-phit-tha-phán	ພິພິດທະພັນ
park (garden)	sǔan sǎa-tháa-la-na	ສວນສາທາລະນະ
police	tạm-lùat	ຕຳຫລວດ
post office	pại-sá-níi (hóhng sǎai)	ໄປສະນີ (ໂຮງສາຍ)
public telephone	thóh-la-sáp sǎa-tháa-la-na	ໂທລະສັບ ສາທາລະນະ
public toilet	hàwng nâm sǎa-tháa-la-na	ຫ້ອງນ້ຳ ສາທາລະນະ
school	hóhng hían	ໂຮງຮຽນ
telephone centre	sǔun thóh-la-sáp	ສູນໂທລະສັບ
tourist information office	hàwng khàw múun khao sǎan thawng thiaw	ຫ້ອງຂໍ້ ມູນຂ່າວສານ ທ່ອງທ່ຽວ

AT THE BANK ຢູ່ທະນາຄານ

The official national currency in the LPDR is the kip (ກີບ, kìip). In reality, the people of Laos use three currencies in day-to-day commerce: kip, Thai baht and US dollars. Kip notes come in denominations of 100, 500, 1000, 2000 and 5000.

By and large, the best exchange rates are available at banks rather than moneychangers. Travellers cheques receive a slightly better exchange rate than cash. Banks in larger towns can change Euros, Canadian, US and Australian dollars, French francs, Thai baht and Japanese yen, while provincial banks will accept only US dollars or baht.

Many hotels, upscale restaurants and gift shops in Vientiane and Luang Prabang accept Visa or MasterCard. A few also accept American Express.

I want to change money.
khàwy yàak pian ngóen — ຂ້ອຍຢາກປ່ຽນເງິນ

Can I/we change money here?
pian ngóen yuu nîi dâi baw — ປ່ຽນເງິນຢູ່ນີ້ໄດ້ບໍ່

What is the exchange rate?
át-tạa lâek pian thao dại — ອັດຕາແລກປ່ຽນເທົ່າໃດ

Can I get smaller change?
khǎw pian ngóen nâwy dâi baw — ຂໍປ່ຽນເງິນນ້ອຍໄດ້ບໍ່

I want to change ...	khàwy yàak pian ...	ຂ້ອຍຢາກປ່ຽນ ...
cash/money	ngóen sót/ngóen	ເງິນສົດ/ເງິນ
a cheque	bại saek	ໃບແຊັກ
a travellers cheque	saek thawng thiaw	ແຊັກທ່ອງທ່ຽວ

Can I use my credit card to withdraw money?
khàwy sâi bát khléh-dít thǎwn ngóen dâi baw — ຂ້ອຍໃຊ້ບັດຄຣເດິດ ຖອນເງິນໄດ້ບໍ່

What's your commission?
jâo ào khâa bàw-li-kàan thao dại — ເຈົ້າເອົາຄ່າບໍລິການເທົ່າໃດ

How many kip per dollar?
  ják kìip taw dọh-láa — ຈັກກີບ

Can I get smaller change?
  khăw pian ngóen nâwy dâi baw — ຂໍປ່ຽນເງິນນ້ອຍໄດ້ບໍ່

Can I transfer money here from my bank?
  khàwy ọhn ngóen jàak tha-náa-kháan khàwy máa nîi dâi baw — ຂ້ອຍໂອນເງິນຈາກ ທະນາຄານຂ້ອຍ ມານີ້ໄດ້ບໍ່

How many days will it take to arrive?
  ják méu sii máa hâwt — ຈັກມື້ຊິມາຮອດ

Has my money arrived yet?
  ngóen khàwy máa hâwt lâew baw — ເງິນຂ້ອຍມາຮອດແລ້ວບໍ່

Can I transfer money overseas?
  khàwy ọhn ngóen pại taang pá-thêht dâi baw — ຂ້ອຍໂອນເງິນໄປຕ່າງ ປະເທດໄດ້ບໍ່

I have ...	khàwy míi ...	ຂ້ອຍມີ ...
US$	dọh-láa ạa-méh-li-kạa	ໂດລາອາເມລິກາ
UK£	pạwn ạng-kít	ປອນອັງກິດ
A$	dọh-láa ạw-sá-tạa-líi	ໂດລາອົດສຕາລີ
HK$	dọh-láa hong kọng	ໂດລາຮົງກົງ
Euros	yúu-lóh	ຢູໂລ
¥en	yéhn nyii-pun	ເຢັນຍີ່ປຸ່ນ

bank	tha-náa-kháan	ທະນາຄານ
change (n)	ngóen nâwy	ເງິນນ້ອຍ
to change	lâek pian	ແລກປ່ຽນ
check	saek	ແຊັກ
exchange rate	át-tạa lâek pian	ອັດຕາແລກປ່ຽນ
money	ngóen	ເງິນ

AT THE POST OFFICE ຢູ່ຫ້ອງການໄປສະນ

Outgoing mail is fairly reliable and inexpensive. The safe arrival of incoming mail is less certain, especially for packages. When posting any package, even small padded mailers, you must leave the package open for inspection by a postal officer.

Is this the post office?
nîi maen pại-sá-níi baw — ນີ້ແມ່ນໄປສະນີບໍ່

I want to send a ...	khàwy yàak song ...	ຂ້ອຍຢາກສົ່ງ ...
letter	jót-măai	ຈົດໝາຍ
postcard	pại-sá-níi bát	ໄປສະນີບັດ
parcel	haw kheuang	ຫໍ່ເຄື່ອງ
telegram	thóh-la-lêhk	ໂທລະເລກ

Please send it by airmail/surface mail.
ká-lu-náa song tháang ạa-kàat/thám-ma-dáa — ກະລຸນາສົ່ງທາງ ອາກາດ/ທຳມະດາ

How much does it cost to send this to ...?
láa-kháa thao-dai săm-láp song ạn-nîi pại ... — ລາຄາເທົ່າໃດສຳລັບ ສົ່ງອັນນີ້ໄປ ...

May I have (a/an/some) ...?	khăw ...	ຂໍ ...
stamps	sa-taem	ສະແຕມ
envelope	sáwng jót-măai	ຊອງຈົດໝາຍ
insurance	pá-kạn phái	ປະກັນໄພ
registered receipt	bại lóng tha-bịan	ໃບລົງທະບຽນ

This letter is going to the (USA).	
jót-măai nîi pại (ạa-méh-li-kạa)	ຈົດໝາຍນີ້ໄປ ອາເມລິກາ
How much to send this letter to (England)?	
song jót-măai nîi pại (ạng-kít) láa-kháa thao dại	ສົ່ງຈົດໝາຍນີ້ໄປອັງກິດ ລາຄາເທົ່າໃດ
I'd like four 100 kip stamps, please.	
khăw sa-taem bại-la hàwy kìip sii ạn	ຂໍສະແຕມໃບລະ ຮ້ອຍກີບສີອັນ
I want to send this package by air mail.	
khàwy yàak song haw nîi pại tháang ạa-kàat	ຂ້ອຍຢາກສົ່ງຫໍ່ນີ້ໄປ ທາງອາກາດ
I want a registered receipt.	
khàwy yàak dâi bại lóng tha-bịan	ຂ້ອຍຢາກໄດ້ໃບລົງ ທະບຽນ
Where's the poste restante section?	
pawng bạw-li-kạan jót-măai sua kháo yuu săi	ປ່ອງບໍລິການຈົດໝາຍ ຊົ່ວຄາວຢູ່ໃສ
Is there any mail for me?	
míi jót-măai khàwy baw	ມີຈົດໝາຍຂ້ອຍບໍ່
My last name is ...	
náam sá-kụn khàwy máen ...	ນາມສະກຸນຂ້ອຍແມ່ນ ...

Useful Words — ຄຳສັບທີ່ເປັນປະໂຫຍດ

air (mail)	tháang ạa-kàat	ທາງອາກາດ
express (mail)	tháang duan	ທາງດ່ວນ
mail (n)	jót-măai	ຈົດໝາຍ
mail box	tûu jót-măai	ຕູ້ຈົດໝາຍ
postcode	la-hat pại-sa-níi	ລະຫັດໄປສະນີ
to register	lóng tha-bịan	ລົງທະບຽນ
registered mail	jót-măai long tha-bịan	ຈົດໝາຍລົງ ທະບຽນ
surface mail	jót-măai tháang thám-ma-dạa	ຈົດໝາຍທາງ ທຳມະດາ

TELEPHONE ໂທລະສັບ

The best place to make international calls is the International Telephone Office (Cabines Télécommuniques Internationales) on Thanon Setthathirat in Vientiane, which is open 24 hours a day. In provincial capitals, international telephone service is available at the GPO.

international call	thóh-la-sáp la-waang pá-thêht	ໂທລະສັບ ລະຫວ່າງປະເທດ
long distance (domestic)	tháang kại	ທາງໄກ
minute(s)	náa-thíi	ນາທີ
mobile/cell phone	thóh-la-sáp méu thěu	ໂທລະສັບມືຖື
operator	phùu taw sǎai	ຜູ້ຕໍ່ສາຍ
phone book	pêum thóh-la-sáp	ປຶ້ມໂທລະສັບ
phone box	káp thóh-la-sáp	ກັບໂທລະສັບ
phonecard	bát thóh-la-sáp	ບັດໂທລະສັບ
telephone	thóh-la-sáp	ໂທລະສັບ
urgent	duan	ດ່ວນ

How much does it cost to call Australia ...?
thóh-la-sáp pại ạw-sá-tạa-líi láa-kháa thao dại
ໂທລະສັບໄປອົສຕາລີ ລາຄາເທົ່າໃດ

I want to call ...
khàwy yàak thóh ...
ຂ້ອຍຢາກໂທ ...

I'd like to speak for 10 minutes.
khàwy yàak thóh síp náa-thíi
ຂ້ອຍຢາກໂທສິບນາທີ

How much does a (three)-minute call cost?
khaa thóh (sǎam) náa-thíi thao dại
ຄ່າໂທ(ສາມ)ນາທີ ເທົ່າໃດ

How much does each extra minute cost?
kháa thóh phôem náa-thíi la thao dại — ຄ່າໂທເພີ້ມນາທີລະເທົ່າໃດ

The number is ...
bọe thóh maen ... — ເບີໂທແມ່ນ ...

It's engaged.
thóh-la-sáp baw waang — ໂທລະສັບບໍ່ຫ່ວາງ

I've been cut off.
thóh-la-sáp tàt — ໂທລະສັບຕັດ

FAX & TELEGRAPH ໂທລະສານແລະໂທລະເລກ

Fax, telex and telegraph services are handled at the GPO in each provincial capital. Larger hotels with business centres offer the same telecommunication services but always at higher rates.

How much per page?
phaen-la thao dại — ແຜ່ນລະເທົ່າໃດ

How much per word?
khám-la thao dại — ຄໍາລະເທົ່າໃດ

fax	fáek	ແຟັກ
telegraph	thóh-la-lêhk	ໂທລະເລກ

INTERNET ອິນເຕີແນັດ

Is there a local Internet cafe?
míi ịn-tọe-naet kạa-féh baw — ມີອິນເຕີແນັດກາເຟບໍ່

I'd like to get Internet access.
khàwy yàak sâi ịn-tọe-naet — ຂ້ອຍຢາກໃຊ້ອິນເຕີແນັດ

I'd like to check my email.
yàak kùat ịi-máew — ຢາກກວດອີແມວ

I'd like to send an email.
yàak song ịi-máew — ຢາກສົ່ງອີແມວ

computer	kháwm-pịi-tọe	ຄອມປີເຕີ
email	ịi-máew	ອີແມວ
modem	móh-dạem	ໂມແດມ

PAPERWORK ເອກະສານ

name	seu	ຊື່
address	thii yuu	ທີ່ຢູ່
date of birth	wán dẹuan pị kòet	ວັນເດືອນປີເກີດ
place of birth	thii kòet	ທີ່ເກີດ
age	ạa-nyu	ອາຍຸ
sex	phêht	ເພດ
nationality	săn-sâat	ສັນຊາດ
religion	sàat-sá-náa	ສາສະນາ
profession/work	ạa-sîip	ອາຊີບ
reason for travel	jút-pa-sŏng dọen tháang	ຈຸດປະສົງເດີນທາງ
customs	dàan pháa-sĭi	ດ່ານພາສີ
marital status	thăa-na kạan taeng-ngáan	ຖານະ ການແຕ່ງງານ
single	sòht	ໂສດ
married	taeng-ngáan lâew	ແຕ່ງງານແລ້ວ
divorced	hâang lâew	ຮ້າງແລ້ວ
widow	mae màai	ແມ່ໝ້າຍ
widower	phaw màai	ພໍ່ໝ້າຍ
identification	bát pá-jạm tụa	ບັດປະຈຳຕົວ
passport number	nâm-bọe năng sĕu phaan dạen	ນຳ້ເບີ ໜັງສືຜ່ານແດນ
visa	wi-sáa	ວີຊາ
drivers licence	bại á-nu-nyâat kháp khii	ໃບອະນຸຍາດຂັບຂີ່
immigration	kùat khón khào méuang	ກວດຄົນເຂົ້າເມືອງ
purpose of visit	jút pa-sŏng yîam yáam	ຈຸດປະສົງຢ້ຽມຢາມ
business	thu-la-kít	ທຸລະກິດ
holiday	phak phawn	ພັກຜ່ອນ
visiting relatives	yáam phii-nâwng	ຢາມພີ່ນ້ອງ
visiting the homeland	yáam bâan kòet	ຢາມບ້ານເກີດ

SIGHTSEEING ການທ່ຽວຊົມ

Where's the tourist office?
hàwng kạan thawng thiaw yuu sǎi
ຫ້ອງການທ່ອງທ່ຽວຢູ່ໃສ

Do you have a local map?
míi phǎen-thii tụa méuang baw
ມີແຜນທີ່ຕົວເມືອງບໍ່

Do you have a guidebook in English?
míi pêum nám thiaw pháa sǎa ạng-kít baw
ມີປື້ມນຳທ່ຽວພາສາອັງກິດບໍ່

What are the main attractions?
laeng thawng thiaw thii sǎm-khán maen nyǎng
ແຫລ່ງທ່ອງທ່ຽວທີ່ສຳຄັນແມ່ນຫຍັງ

Can we take photographs?
thaai hûup dâi baw
ຖ່າຍຮູບໄດ້ບໍ່

I'll send you the photograph.
khàwy síi fàak hûup máa hâi
ຂ້ອຍຊິຝາກຮູບມາໃຫ້

What time does it open/close?
poet/pít wéh-láa ják móhng
ເປີດ/ປິດເວລາຈັກໂມງ

Is there an admission charge?
kép khaa phaan pa-tụu baw
ເກັບຄ່າຜ່ານປະຕູບໍ່

Is there a discount for ...?	lut láa-kháa săm-láp ... baw	ລຸດລາຄາ ສຳລັບ ... ບໍ່
children	dék nâwy	ເດັກນ້ອຍ
students	nak hían	ນັກຮຽນ

What's that building?
nân maen ąa-kháan nyăng — ນັ້ນແມ່ນອາຄານຫຍັງ

What's this monument?
nîi maen ąa-nu-săa-wa-líi nyăng — ນີ້ແມ່ນ ອານຸສາວະລີຫຍັງ

What's that?
nân maen nyăng — ນັ້ນແມ່ນຫຍັງ

How old is it?
ąa-nyu ják pįi lâew — ອາຍຸຈັກປີແລ້ວ

WHAT'S A WAT?

Technically speaking, the wat (ວັດ) is a compound where Buddhist monks and/or nuns reside. In Laos, a typical wat may contain the following structures:

drum tower	hăw kąwng	ຫໍກອງ
ordination hall	sĭm	ສິມ
monastic quarters	kú-tí	ກຸຕິ
stupa	thâat	ທາດ

'bone stupas', where the ashes of worshippers are interred
thâat ká-dùuk — ທາດກະດູກ

pavilion, where laity listen to thám or Buddhist doctrine
săa-láa fáng thám — ສາລາຟັງທຳ

spirit house, for the temple's reigning earth spirit
hăw phĭi khún wat — ຫໍຜີຄຸນວັດ

Tipitaka library, where Buddhist scriptures are stored
hăw tąi — ຫໍໄຕ

Buddhist temple	wat	ວັດ
cave	thám	ຖ້ຳ
memorial	ąa-nu-sǎwn sa-thǎan	ອານຸສອນສະຖານ
museum	phi-phit-tha-phán	ພິພິດທະພັນ
national biodiversity conservation area (NBCA)	khèt á-nu-lak síi-wa-náa-phán haeng sâat	ເຂດອະນຸລັກ ຊີວະນາພັນ ແຫ່ງຊາດ
national park	sǔan ut-thi-yáan haeng sâat	ສວນອຸດທິຍານ ແຫ່ງຊາດ
palace	pha-láa-sa-wáng	ພະລາຊະວັງ
shrine	hǎw wâi	ຫໍໄຫວ້
spirit house	hǎw phǐi	ຫໍຜີ
statue	hûup pân	ຮູບປັ້ນ
stupa	thâat	ທາດ
university	ma-hǎa-wi-tha-nyáa-lái	ມະຫາວິທະຍາໄລ
waterfall	nâm tók tàat	ນ້ຳຕົກຕາດ
zoo	sǔan sát	ສວນສັດ

SIGNS

ຮ້ອນ	HOT
ເຢັນ	COLD
ທາງເຂົ້າ	ENTRANCE
ທາງອອກ	EXIT
ເປີດ	OPEN
ອັດ/ປິດ	CLOSED
ຫ້າມເຂົ້າ	NO ENTRY
ຫ້າມສູບຢາ	NO SMOKING
ຫ້າມ	PROHIBITED
ຫ້ອງນ້ຳ	TOILETS

WAT'S THE STORY?

Correct behaviour in a wat entails several guidelines, the most important of which is to dress neatly (no shorts or sleeveless shirts) and to take your shoes off when you enter any building that contains a Buddha image. Buddha images are sacred objects, so don't pose in front of them for pictures and definitely do not clamber upon them.

Monks are not supposed to touch or be touched by women. If a woman wants to hand something to a monk, the object should be placed within reach of the monk, not handed directly to him.

When sitting in a religious edifice, keep your feet pointed away from any Buddha images or monks. The usual way to do this is to sit in the 'mermaid' pose in which your legs are folded to the side, with the feet pointing backwards.

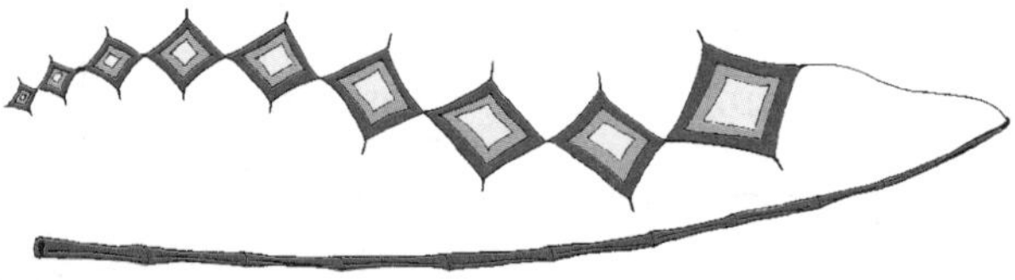

BARGAINING ການຕໍ່ລອງລາຄາ

Negotiating prices, ie, bargaining, is a common practice in Laos, as in most of South-East Asia. You can expect to bargain for most items offered for sale in a market, even when prices are posted. In department stores and convenience shops, however, prices are fixed. Don't go overboard when bargaining – both seller and buyer lose face when you argue too vehemently or haggle over a few kìip (ກີບ).

How much?	thao dại	ເທົ່າໃດ
How many kip?	ják kìip	ຈັກກີບ

Do you have something cheaper?
míi aạn thèuk-kwaa nîi baw — ມີອັນຖືກກ່ວານີ້ບໍ່

The price is very high.
láa-kháa pháeng lǎai — ລາຄາແພງຫລາຍ

I think that's too much.
khit waa pháeng phôht — ຄິດວ່າແພງໂພດ

Can you bring the price down?
lut láa-kháa dâi baw — ລຸດລາຄາໄດ້ບໍ່

Can you lower it more?
lut ìik dâi baw — ລຸດອີກໄດ້ບໍ່

How about ... kip?
... kìip dâi baw — ... ກີບໄດ້ບໍ່

I don't have much money.
khàwy baw míi ngóen lǎai — ຂ້ອຍບໍ່ມີເງິນຫລາຍ

If I/we buy two ... (+ classifier) will you lower the price?
thàa sêu sǎwng ... lut dâi baw — ຖ້າຊື້ສອງ ... ລຸດໄດ້ບໍ່

The quality is not very good.
khún-na-phâap baw dịi pạan dại — ຄຸນນະພາບບໍ່ດີປານໃດ

What's your lowest price?
láa-kháa tam sút thao dại — ລາຄາຕໍ່າສຸດເທົ່າໃດ

MAKING A PURCHASE ການຈັດຊ

Do you have any ...?	mii ... baw	ມີ ... ບໍ່
Please give me ...	khăw ...	ຂໍ ...
I'm looking for ...	khàwy sàwk hăa ...	ຂອຍຊອກຫາ ...
Do you have any more?	mii ìik baw	ມີອີກບໍ່
I'd like to see another style.	khăw boeng ìik bàep neung	ຂໍເບິ່ງອີກແບບໜຶ່ງ

How much (for) ...?	... thao dai	... ເທົ່າໃດ
both	tháng săwng	ທັງສອງ
per fruit	nuay-la	ໜ່ວຍລະ
per metre	maet-la	ແມັດລະ
per piece	an-la	ອັນລະ
this	an-nîi	ອັນນີ້
three pieces	săam an	ສາມອັນ

How much altogether?
thuk yaang thao dai ທຸກຢ່າງເທົ່າໃດ

SHOPPING

I'd like (a) ...	khàwy tâwng-kąan ...	ຂ້ອຍຕ້ອງການ ...
Where can	já hǎa ...	ຈະຫາ ...
I find (a) ...?	dâi yuu sǎi	ໄດ້ຢູ່ໃສ
batteries	thaan fái sǎai	ຖ່ານໄຟສາຍ
bread	khào jii	ເຂົ້າຈີ່
butter	bǫe	ເບີ
candles	thían	ທຽນ
cheese	nóei khǎeng	ເນີຍແຂງ
chocolate	sawk-kǫh-laet	ຊັອກໂກແລັດ
eggs	khai	ໄຂ່
flour	pâeng	ແປ້ງ
gas cylinder	thǎng káet	ຖັງແກສ
ham	háem	ແຮມ
honey	nâm phòeng	ນ້ຳເຜີ້ງ
margarine	mâak-kąa-lín	ມາກກາລິນ

matches	káp-khìit	ກັບຂີດ
milk	nâm nóm	ນ້ຳນົມ
mosquito coil	yąa jùt nyúng	ຢາຈູດຍຸງ
mosquito repellant	yąa kąn nyúng	ຢາກັນຍຸງ
pepper	màak phét	ໝາກເຜັດ
salt	kęua	ເກືອ
shampoo	yąa sa hǔa	ຢາຊະຫົວ
soap	sá-bųu	ສະບູ
sugar	nâm tąan	ນ້ຳຕານ
toilet paper	jîa hàwng nâm	ເຈ້ຍຫ້ອງນ້ຳ
toothpaste	yąa thǔu khàew	ຢາຖູແຂ້ວ
washing powder	fâep	ແຟບ

SOUVENIRS & CRAFTS ເຄື່ອງທີ່ລະລຶກແລະເຄື່ອງຫັດຖະກຳ

Hill-tribe crafts abound in Laos, and make fine souvenirs of your travels. Like elsewhere in South-East Asia, bargaining is a local tradition (originally introduced to the area by early Arab and Indian traders). Although most shops nowadays have fixed prices, fabric, carvings, jewellery and antiques are usually subject to bargaining.

The Lao produce well-crafted carvings in wood, bone and stone. Subjects can be anything from Hindu or Buddhist mythology to themes from everyday life. Opium pipes seem to be plentiful in Laos and sometimes have intricately carved bone or bamboo shafts, along with engraved ceramic bowls. Vientiane, Luang Prabang, Pakse and Savannakhet each have a sprinkling of antique shops. Anything that looks old could be up for sale in these shops, including Asian pottery (especially Ming dynasty porcelain), old jewellery, clothes, carved wood, musical instruments, coins and bronze statuettes.

baskets	ká-taa	ກະຕ່າ
handicrafts	kheuang hát-thá-kạm	ເຄື່ອງຫັດຖະກຳ
pottery/ceramics	kheuang dìn	ເຄື່ອງດິນ

MATERIALS ວັດຖຸ

What is this made of?
nîi het dûay nyǎng ນີ້ເຮັດດ້ວຍຫຍັງ

aluminium	áa-lúu-míi-níam	ອາລູມີນຽມ
brass	tháwng lěuang	ທອງເຫລືອງ
bronze	tháwng sǎm-lit	ທອງສຳລິດ
cloth	phàa	ຜ້າ
copper	tháwng dạeng	ທອງແດງ
gold (pure)	khám	ຄຳ

gold-plated	khám bại	ຄຳໃບ
leather	nǎng	ໜັງ
silver	ngóen	ເງິນ
stone	hǐn	ຫີນ
teak	mâi sák	ໄມ້ສັກ
wood	mâi	ໄມ້

LAO LOOMS

All together Laos is said to have some 16 basic weaving styles divided among four basic regions. Southern weavers, who often use foot looms rather than frame looms, practise Laos' most continuous textile traditions in terms of styles and patterns, some of which haven't changed for a century or more. Southern Laos is known for the best silk weaving and for intricate mat-mịi (ikat or tie-dye) designs that include Khmer-influenced temple and elephant motifs. Synthetic and natural dyes are commonly used.

In north-eastern Laos (especially Hua Phan's Sam Neua and Xieng Khuang's Muang Phuan) the Thai Neua, Phuan, Thai Lü, Thai Daeng, Thai Dam and Phu Thai mainly produce weft brocade (yìap kọ) using raw silk, cotton yarn and natural dyes, sometimes with the addition of mat-mịi techniques. Large diamond patterns are common.

In central Laos, typical weavings include indigo-dyed cotton mat-míi and minimal weft brocade (jók and khít), along with techniques borrowed from all over the country (brought by migrants to Vientiane – many of whom fled war zones). Gold and silver brocade is typical of traditional Luang Prabang patterns, along with intricate patterns (lái) and imported Thai Lü designs.

Northerners generally use frame looms; the waist, body and bottom border of a phàa nung or sarong are often sewn together from separately woven pieces.

TEXTILES ຜ້າແພ

Silk and cotton fabrics are woven in many different styles according to the geographic provenance and ethnicity of the weavers.

cotton	phàa fâai	ຜ້າຝ້າຍ
embroidery	phàa thák saew	ຜ້າທັກແສ່ວ
ikat-style tie-dyed cloth	mat-mii	ມັດໝີ່
minimal weft brocade	jók/khít	ຈົກ/ຂິດ
silk	phàa măi	ຜ້າໄໝ
shoulder bag	thŏng pháai	ຖົງພາຍ
traditional long sarong for women	sìin	ສິ້ນ

GEMS & JEWELLERY ເພັດພອຍ ແລະ ເຄື່ອງປະດັບ

Gold and silver jewellery is a good buy in Laos, although you must search hard for well-made pieces. Some of the best silverwork is done by the hill tribes. Gems are also sometimes available, but you can get better prices in Thailand.

Most provincial towns have a few shops that specialise in jewellery. You can also find jewellery in antique and handicraft shops.

bracelet	săi khăen	ສາຍແຂນ
diamond	phet	ເພັດ
emerald	kâew máw-la-kót	ແກ້ວມໍລະກົດ
gems	phet pháwy	ເພັດພອຍ
jade	nyók	ຫຍົກ
necklace	săai kháw	ສາຍຄໍ
ring	wăen	ແຫວນ
ruby	thap thím	ທັບທິມ
sapphire	pháwy sĭi kháam	ພອຍສີຄາມ
silver	ngóen	ເງິນ

CLOTHING — ເຄື່ອງ

The general Lao word for clothing is sèua phàa (ເສື້ອຜ້າ). Sèua (ເສື້ອ) itself can mean 'shirt', 'blouse', 'dress' or 'jacket'; phàa (ຜ້າ) means 'cloth'.

hat	mùak	ໝວກ
shirt/blouse/ jacket/dress	sèua	ເສື້ອ
shoes	kòep	ເກີບ
skirt (Lao-style)	sìin	ສິ້ນ
skirt (Western-style)	ká-pohng	ກະໂປ່ງ
socks	thŏng thâo	ຖົງເທົ້າ
style	bàep	ແບບ
tailor	saang tát kheuang	ຊ່າງຕັດເຄື່ອງ
trousers	sòng khăa nyáo	ສົ້ງຂາຍາວ
underwear	sòng sâwn	ສົ້ງຊ້ອນ
Can you make ...?	tát ... dâi baw	ຕັດ ... ໄດ້ບໍ່
The sleeves are too ...	khăen ... phôht	ແຂນ ... ໂພດ
long	nyáo	ຍາວ
short	sàn	ສັ້ນ

FABRICS — ຜ້າ

Synthetic materials and Western fabric weaves use the same names as in English (eg, polyester, dacron, serge, gabardine, etc), spoken with a Lao accent.

cotton	phàa fàai	ຜ້າຝ້າຍ
leather	năng	ໜັງ
linen	phàa lîi-nín	ຜ້າລີນິນ
silk	phàa măi	ຜ້າໄໝ
wool	phàa khŏn sát	ຜ້າຂົນສັດ

COLOURS ສີ

dark	sǐi kae	ສີແກ່
light	sǐi awn	ສີອ່ອນ
black	sǐi dạm	ສີດຳ
blue	sǐi fâa	ສີຟ້າ
brown	sǐi nâm-tạan	ສີນ້ຳຕານ
green	sǐi khǐaw	ສີຂຽວ
grey	sǐi khìi thao	ສີຂີ້ເທົ່າ
pink	sǐi bụa	ສີບົວ
purple	sǐi muang	ສີມ່ວງ
red	sǐi dạeng	ສີແດງ
white	sǐi khǎo	ສີຂາວ
yellow	sǐi lěuang	ສີເຫລືອງ

Do you have another colour?
míi sǐi eun baw — ມີສີອື່ນບໍ່

TOILETRIES ເຄື່ອງສຳອາງ

brush	pạeng	ແປງ
comb	wǐi	ຫວີ
condoms	thǒng yạang á-náa-mái	ຖົງຢາງອະນາໄມ
dental floss	sêuak jîim khàew	ເຊືອກຈີ້ມແຂ້ວ
deodorant	yạa kạn kin tụa	ຢາກັນກິ່ນຕົວ
moisturiser	khíim tháa nàa	ຄີມທາໜ້າ
razor	mîit thǎe	ມີດແຖ
razor blades	bại mîit thǎe	ໃບມີດແຖ
sanitary napkins	phàa á-náa-mái	ຜ້າອະນາໄມ
shampoo	nâm yạa sá phǒm	ນ້ຳຢາຊະຜົມ
shaving cream	yáa thǎe nùat	ຢາແຖໜວດ
soap	sá-bụu	ສະບູ
sunblock	yáa kạn dàet	ຢາກັນແດດ
tissues	jîa á-náa-mái	ເຈ້ຍອະນາໄມ
toilet paper	jîa hàwng nâm	ເຈ້ຍຫ້ອງນ້ຳ
toothbrush	pạeng thǔu khàew	ແປງຖູແຂ້ວ
toothpaste	yạa thǔu khàew	ຢາຖູແຂ້ວ

STATIONERY & PUBLICATIONS — ເຈ້ຍແລະສິ່ງພິມ

book	pêum	ປຶ້ມ
bookshop	hàan khǎai pêum	ຮ້ານຂາຍປຶ້ມ
envelope	sáwng jót-mǎai	ຊອງຈິດໝາຍ
guidebook	pêum thawng thiaw	ປຶ້ມທ່ອງທ່ຽວ
ink	nâm móek	ນ້ຳເມິກ
magazine	wáa-la-sǎan	ວາລະສານ
newspaper	nǎng-sěu phím	ໜັງສືພິມ
notebook	pêum bạn théuk	ປຶ້ມບັນທຶກ
pen	bík	ບິກ
pencil	sǎw dạm	ສໍດຳ
stationery	keuang khǐan	ເຄື່ອງຂຽນ
writing paper	jîa khǐan	ເຈ້ຍຂຽນ

PHOTOGRAPHY — ການຖ່າຍຮູບ

camera	kâwng thaai hûup	ກ້ອງຖ່າຍຮູບ
develop (photos)	lâang hûup	ລ້າງຮູບ
lens	léhn	ເລນ
photograph	hûup	ຮຸບ
to photograph	thaai hûup	ຖາຍຮູບ
film	fím hûup	ຟິມຮູບ
colour	fím sǐi	ຟິມສີ
B&W	fím khǎo dạm	ຟິມຂາວດຳ
slide film	fím sá-lái	ຟິມສະໄລ

When will it be ready?
wéh-láa-dại já lâang hûup jóp lâew — ເວລາໃດຈະລ້າງ ຮູບຈົບແລ້ວ

How many days?
ják mêu — ຈັກມື້

SMOKING ສູບຢາ

A packet of ... cigarettes, please.
  ạo yạa sùup hài dae sáwng nèung — ເອົາຢາສູບໃຫ້ແດ່ ຊອງໜຶ່ງ

Are these cigarettes strong or mild?
  yạa nîi púk lěu jạang — ຢານີ້ປຸກຫລືຈາງ

Do you have a light?
  míi káp fái baw — ມີກັບໄຟບໍ່

Please don't smoke.
  ká-lu-náa yạa sùup yáa — ກະລຸນາຢ່າສູບຢາ

Can I smoke?
  sùup yạa dâi baw — ສູບຢາໄດ້ບໍ່

cigarettes	yạa sùup	ຢາສູບ
cigarette papers	jîa phán yạa sùup	ເຈັ້ຍພັນຢາສູບ
filtered	kạwng	ກອງ
lighter	káp fái	ກັບໄຟ
matches	káp khìit	ກັບຂີດ
menthol	yáa sùup yén	ຢາສູບເຢັນ
pipe	kàwk	ກອກ
tobacco	yáa sèn	ຢາເສັ້ນ

ONE LOH OF BREAD

Don't forget to use a classifier when indicating a number of something – the general-purpose classifier that should get you through is loh. Find more classifiers on page 43.

WEIGHTS & MEASURES ການຊັ່ງແລະການວັດແທກ

Dimensions and weight are usually expressed using the metric system in Laos. The exception is land measure, which is usually quoted using the traditional system of wáa, ngáan and hâi. Gold jewellery is often measured in baht (bàat).

1 wáa	= 4 sq metres	ວາ
1 ngáan (100 sq wáa)	= 400 sq metres	ງານ
1 hâi (4 ngáan)	= 1600 sq metres	ໄຮ່
1 bàat	= 15 grams	ບາດ

kilogram	kí-lóh	ກິໂລ
kilometre	kí-lóh-maet	ກິໂລແມັດ
metre	maet	ແມັດ
litre	liit	ລິດ

SIZES & COMPARISONS ຂະໜາດແລະການສິມທຽບ

Do you have anything ... than this?	míi ... nîi baw	ມີ ... ນີ້ບໍ່
larger	nyai-kwaa	ໃຫຍ່ກ່ວາ
smaller	nâwy-kwaa	ນ້ອຍກ່ວາ

too tight	kháp phôht	ຄັບໂພດ
too small	nâwy phôht	ນ້ອຍໂພດ
too large	nyai phôht	ໃຫຍ່ໂພດ
too wide	kwâang phôht	ກ້ວາງໂພດ
too long	nyáo phôht	ຍາວໂພດ
too short	sàn phôht	ສັ້ນໂພດ

to bargain	taw	ຕໍ່
to buy	sêu	ຊື້
cheap	thèuk	ຖືກ
expensive	pháeng	ແພງ
quality	khún-na-phâap	ຄຸນນະພາບ
sell	khăai	ຂາຍ
size	kha-nàat	ຂະໜາດ
not enough	baw pháw	ບໍ່ພໍ
still not enough	nyáng baw pháw	ຍັງບໍ່ພໍ
good enough	pháw dịi	ພໍດີ
I'd like to see ...	yàak boeng ...	ຢາກເບິ່ງ ...
this one	ạn nîi	ອັນນີ້
that one	ạn nân	ອັນນັ້ນ

Which one?
ạn dại — ອັນໃດ

Do you have any more?
míi iik baw — ມີອີກບໍ່

Lao cuisine is similar to Thai cuisine in many ways. Almost all dishes are cooked using fresh ingredients, including vegetables, fish, poultry, pork and beef or water buffalo.

Except for one-dish rice plates and noodle dishes, Lao meals are usually ordered family style, which is to say that two or more people order together, sharing different dishes. Traditionally, the party orders one of each kind of dish, eg, one salad, one stir-fry, one soup, etc. Each dish is generally large enough for two people. Extras may be ordered for a large party.

Because of Laos' distance from the sea, freshwater fish is more commonly used than saltwater fish or shellfish. To salt the food, various fermented fish concoctions are used, most commonly **nâm pąa** (ນ້ຳປາ), which is a thin sauce of fermented anchovies (usually imported from Thailand), and **pąa dàek** (ປາແດກ), a coarser, native Lao preparation that includes chunks of fermented freshwater fish, rice husks and rice 'dust'. **Nâm pąa dàek** (ນ້ຳປາແດກ) is the sauce poured from **pąa dàek**.

Many Lao dishes are quite spicy because of the Lao penchant for chillies or **màak phét** (ໝາກເຜັດ). But the Lao also eat a lot of what could be called Chinese food which is generally, but not always, less spicy.

Rice is the foundation for all Lao meals (as opposed to snacks), as elsewhere in South-East Asia. In general, the Lao eat 'sticky' or glutinous rice (ເຂົ້າໜຽວ, **khào nǐaw**), although ordinary steamed white rice (ເຂົ້າໜຶ້ງ, **khào nèung**) is also common. Sticky rice is served in lidded baskets and eaten with the hands: the general practice is to grab a small fistful from the woven container that sits on the table, then roll it into a rough ball which is used to dip into the various dishes. **Khào nèung**, on the other hand, is eaten with a fork and spoon. The fork is only used to prod food onto the spoon, which is the main utensil for eating this type of rice. Chopsticks (ໄມ້ທູ່, **mâi thuu**) are only used for eating **fõe** (ເຝີ) or other Chinese noodle dishes.

AT THE RESTAURANT ຢູ່ຮ້ານອາຫານ

Please bring (a) ...	khăw ... dae	ຂໍ ... ແດ່
bill	saek	ແຊັກ
bowl	thùay	ຖ້ວຍ
chopsticks	mâi thuu	ໄມ້ທູ່
fork	sâwm	ສ້ອມ
glass	jàwk	ຈອກ
knife	mîit	ມີດ
menu	láai-kąan ąa-hăan	ລາຍການອາຫານ
plate	jąan	ຈານ
spoon	buang	ບ່ວງ

I don't like it hot and spicy.
baw mak phét ບໍ່ມັກເຜັດ

I like it hot and spicy.
mak phét ມັກເຜັດ

I can eat Lao food.
kįn ąa-hăan láo dâi ກິນອາຫານລາວໄດ້

Do you have ...?
míi ... baw ມີ ... ບໍ່

What do you have that's special?
míi nyăng phi-sèt baw ມີຫຍັງພິເສດບໍ່

I'd like to try that.
khàwy yàak láwng kįn boeng ຂ້ອຍຢາກລອງກິນເບິ່ງ

I didn't order this.
khàwy baw dâi sang náew nîi ຂ້ອຍບໍ່ໄດ້ສັ່ງແນວນີ້

delicious sâep ແຊບ

WIT & WISDOM

It's easy to earn money but difficult to find kindness.

ngóen khám hăa dâi, ເງິນຄຳຫາໄດ້
nâm jąi hăa yàak ນ້ຳໃຈຫາຫຍາກ

VEGETARIAN MEALS ອາຫານເຈ

Those visitors who wish to avoid eating animal food while in Laos can be accommodated only with extreme effort. Chinese restaurants are your best bet since many Chinese Buddhists eat vegetarian food during Buddhist festivals. More often than not, however, visiting vegetarians are left to their own devices at the average restaurant. In Lao the magic words are:

I eat only vegetables.
    khàwy kịn tae phák — ຂ້ອຍກິນແຕ່ຜັກ

I can't eat pork.
    khàwy kịn mŭu baw dâi — ຂ້ອຍກິນຊີ້ນໝູບໍ່ໄດ້

I can't eat beef.
    khàwy kịn sìin ngúa baw dâi — ຂ້ອຍກິນງົວບໍ່ໄດ້

I don't want any meat.
    khàwy baw ạo sìin sát — ຂ້ອຍບໍ່ເອົາຊີ້ນສັດ

No fish or chicken.
    baw sai pạa lĕu kai — ບໍ່ໃສ່ປາຫລືໄກ່

I/We want vegetables only.
(see Vegetables, page 111)
    ạo phák thao nân — ເອົາຜັກເທົ່ານັ້ນ

Please don't use fish sauce.
    ká-lu-náa baw sai nâm pạa — ກະລຸນາບໍ່ໃສ່ນ້ຳປາ

Please don't use padaek.
    ká-lu-náa baw sai pạa dàek — ກະລຸນາບໍ່ໃສ່ປາແດກ

Please don't use MSG.
    ká-lu-náa baw sai pâeng núa — ກະລຸນາບໍ່ໃສ່ແປ້ງນົວ

soy sauce	nâm sá-îu	ນ້ຳສະອິ້ວ
tofu (soybean curd)	tâo-hûu	ເຕົາຮູ້
vegetable oil	nâm-mán phêut	ນ້ຳມັນພືດ

FOOD

STAPLES ກາລາເຟ

beef	sìin ngúa	ຊີ້ນງົວ
chicken	kai	ໄກ່
fish	pạa	ປາ
pork	sìin mŭu	ຊີ້ນໝູ
rice	khào	ເຂົ້າ
seafood	ạa-hăan tha-léh	ອາຫານທະເລ
shrimp/prawns	kûng	ກຸ້ງ
vegetables	phak	ຜັກ
water buffalo	sìin khuáai	ຊີ້ນຄວາຍ

RICE DISHES ອາຫານກັບເຂົ້າ

steamed white rice	khào nèung	ເຂົ້າໜຶ້ງ
sticky rice	khào nĭaw	ເຂົ້າໜຽວ
curry over rice	khào làat kạeng	ເຂົ້າລາດແກງ
'red' pork (char siu) with rice	khào mŭu dạeng	ເຂົ້າໝູແດງ
roast duck over rice	khào nàa pét	ເຂົ້າໜ້າເປັດ
fried rice with ...	khào phát (khào khùa) ...	ເຂົ້າຜັດ (ເຂົ້າຂົ້ວ) ...
chicken	kai	ໄກ່
pork	mŭu	ໝູ
shrimp/prawns	kûng	ກຸ້ງ
crab	pụu	ປູ

NOODLES ເຝີ/ໝີ່

Fŏe (ເຝີ), perhaps the most common food sold anywhere in Laos, are flat noodles made with rice flour. Heavier wheat noodles – sometimes made with egg, sometimes not – are known as mii (ໝີ່). You'll find both kinds noodles in most Lao restaurants and in small hàan fŏe (noodle shops). Slivers of beef or pork are the usual accompaniments, though occasionally chicken may be available. Because of their Chinese origins, noodles are usually eaten with chopsticks (and a spoon if served in a broth).

Fŏe is quite popular as a snack or even for breakfast, and is almost always served with a plate of fresh lettuce, mint, coriander, mung-bean sprouts, lime wedges and sometimes basil, for adding to the soup as desired. In some places – especially in the south – people mix their own fŏe sauce of lime, crushed fresh chilli, fermented shrimp paste (ກະປິ, ká-pí) and sugar at the table using a little saucer provided for that purpose.

fŏe ເຝີ
rice noodle soup with vegetables and meat

fŏe hàeng ເຝີແຫ້ງ
rice noodles with vegetables and meat, no broth

làat nàa ລາດໜ້າ
rice noodles with gravy

fŏe khùa ເຝີຂົ້ວ
fried rice noodles with meat and vegetables

phát sá-îu ຜັດສະອິ້ວ
fried rice noodles with soy sauce

mii nâm ໝີ່ນ້ຳ
yellow wheat noodles in broth, with vegetables and meat

mii hàeng ໝີ່ແຫ້ງ
yellow wheat noodles with vegetables and meat

khào pûn ເຂົ້າປຸ້ນ
white flour noodles served with sweet-spicy sauce

BREAD & PASTRIES — ເຂົ້າຈີ່ ແລະ ເຂົ້າໜົມ

plain bread (usually French-style)
khào jii — ເຂົ້າຈີ່

baguette sandwich
khào jii páa-tê — ເຂົ້າຈີ່ປາເຕ

croissants
khúa-sawng — ຄົວຊ່ອງ

'Chinese doughnuts'
(Mandarin youtiao)
pá-thawng-kó
(khào-nǒm khuu) — ປະຖ່ອງໂກະ (ເຂົ້າໜົມຄູ່)

EGGS — ໄຂ່

egg	khai	ໄຂ່
fried egg	khai dạo	ໄຂ່ດາວ
hard-boiled egg	khai tôm	ໄຂ່ຕົ້ມ
plain omelette	jẹun khai	ຈືນໄຂ່
scrambled egg	khai khùa	ໄຂ່ຂົ້ວ

APPETISERS ('DRINKING FOOD') — ກັບແກ້ມ

Káp kâem (ກັບແກ້ມ) are dishes intended to be eaten on picnics or while drinking beer, lào láo (ເຫຼົ້າລາວ, rice alcohol) or other alcoholic beverages. English-language menus in Laos may translate such dishes as 'snacks' or 'appetisers'. You can also order káp kâem with regular meals, although they will usually be served before other kinds of dishes.

cellophane noodle salad	yám sèn wûn	ຍຳເສັ້ນຫວຸ້ນ
dried water buffalo skin	nǎng khuáai hàeng	ໜັງຄວາຍແຫ້ງ
fried peanuts	thua dịn jẹun	ຖົ່ວດິນຈືນ
fried potatoes	mán fa-lang jẹun	ມັນຝລັ່ງຈືນ

fresh spring rolls	yáw díp	ຢໍດິບ
fried spring rolls	yáw jẹun	ຢໍຈືນ
shrimp chips	khào khìap kûng	ເຂົ້າຂຽບກຸ້ງ
spicy green papaya salad	tạm màak-hung	ຕຳໝາກຫຸ່ງ
spicy grilled chicken	pîng kai	ປີ້ງໄກ່
toasted pork	pîng mǔu	ປີ້ງໝູ

MEAT SALADS ລາບ

One of the most common Lao dishes is làap (ລາບ), which is a salad of minced meat, chicken or fish tossed with lime juice, garlic, khào khùa (ເຂົ້າຂົ້ວ, roast, powdered sticky rice), green onions, mint leaves and chillies. It can be very hot or rather mild, depending on the cook or your own request. Làap is typically served with a large plate of lettuce, mint and steamed mango leaves. Using your fingers, you wrap a little làap in the lettuce and herbs and eat it with hand-rolled balls of sticky rice.

beef laap	làap sìin	ລາບຊີ້ນ
chicken laap	làap kai	ລາບໄກ່
fish laap	làap pạa	ລາບປາ
pork laap	làap mǔu	ລາບໝູ

SOUP ແກງ

fish and lemongrass soup with mushrooms
tôm yám pạa — ຕົ້ມຍຳປາ

mild soup with vegetables and pork
kạeng jèut — ແກງຈືດ

same as above, with bean curd
kạeng jèut tâo-hûu — ແກງຈືດເຕົາຮູ້

rice soup with ...	khào pìak ...	ເຂົ້າປຽກ ...
chicken	kai	ໄກ່
fish	pạa	ປາ
pork	mǔu	ໝູ

STIR-FRIED DISHES ຂົ້ວ-ອາຫານປະເພດຂົ້ວ

beef in oyster sauce	
ngúa phàt nâm-mán hǎwy	ງົວຜັດນ້ຳມັນຫອຍ
chicken with ginger	
kai phát khǐing	ໄກ່ຜັດຂີງ
chicken fried with chillies	
kai phát màak phét	ໄກ່ຜັດໝາກເຜັດ
chicken with mushrooms	
kai phát hét	ໄກ່ຜັດເຫັດ
stir-fried mixed vegetables	
phát phák	ຜັດຜັກ
sweet and sour pork	
mǔu sòm-wǎan	ໝູສົ້ມຫວານ

FISH ປາ

crisp-fried fish	jẹun pạa	ຈືນປາ
fried prawns	jẹun kûng	ຈືນກຸ້ງ
grilled prawns	pîing kûng	ປີ້ງກຸ້ງ
steamed fish	nèung pạa	ໜຶ້ງປາ
grilled fish	pîing pạa	ປີ້ງປາ
sweet & sour fish	pạa sòm-wǎan	ປາສົ້ມຫວານ
catfish	pạa dúk	ປາດຸກ
carp	pạa pàak	ປາປາກ
eel	ian	ອ່ຽນ
freshwater stingray	pạa fǎa lái	ປາຝາໄລ
giant Mekong catfish	pạa béuk	ປາບຶກ
serpent fish	pạa khaw	ປາຄໍ່
sheatfish	pạa sa-ngûa	ປາສະງົ້ວ

VEGETABLES — ຜັກ

bamboo shoots	naw mâi	ໜໍ່ໄມ້
bean	thua	ຖົ່ວ
bean sprouts	thua ngâwk	ຖົ່ວງອກ
bitter melon	máa-láa-jịin (màak ha)	ມາລາຈີນ (ໝາກຣະ)
cabbage	ká-lam pịi	ກະລໍາປີ
cauliflower	ká-lam pịi dàwk	ກະລໍາປີດອກ
Chinese radish (daikon)	phák kàat hŭa	ຜັກກາດຫົວ
corn	khào săa-líi	ເຂົ້າສາລີ
cucumber	màak tạeng	ໝາກແຕງ
eggplant	màak khĕua	ໝາກເຂືອ
garlic	hŭa phák thíam	ຫົວຜັກທຽມ
lettuce	phák sá-lat	ຜັກສະລັດ
long green beans	thua nyáo	ຖົ່ວຍາວ
lotus root	tôn bụa	ຕົ້ນບົວ
onion	hŭa phák bua	ຫົວຜັກບົ່ວ
onion (green 'scallions')	tôn phák bua	ຕົ້ນຜັກບົ່ວ
peanuts	màak thua dịn	ໝາກຖົ່ວດິນ
potato	mán fa-lang	ມັນຝລັ່ງ
pumpkin	màak éu (màak fák)	ໝາກອຶ (ໝາກຟັກ)
tomato	màak len	ໝາກເລັ່ນ

WIT & WISDOM

When choosing an elephant, check the tail;
when choosing a wife, look at her mother.

lêuak sang hài boeng hăang, ເລືອກຊ້າງໃຫ້ເບິ່ງຫາງ
lêuak náan hài boeng mae ເລືອກນາງໃຫ້ເບິ່ງແມ່

FOOD

CONDIMENTS, HERBS & SPICES

ເຄື່ອງປຸງ, ເຄື່ອງຫອມແລະເຄື່ອງເທດ

Along with chillies, lime juice, lemon grass and fresh coriander leaf are added to give Lao food its characteristic tang. Nâm pạa (ນ້ຳປາ), a thin, clear fish sauce made from fermented anchovies, or ká-pí, fermented shrimp paste, provide the cuisine's main salty element.

Other common seasonings include hot chillies, ground peanuts, tamarind juice, lime juice, ginger and coconut milk. Chillies are sometimes served on the side in hot pepper sauces called jaew (ແຈ່ວ).

Granulated salt and ground black pepper are almost never present on a Lao table, although they may be used during the cooking. Soy sauce can be requested, though this is normally used as a condiment for Chinese food only.

chilli	màak phét	ໝາກເຜັດ
coconut extract	nâm ká-thí	ນ້ຳກະທິ
coriander (cilantro)	phák hǎwm	ຜັກຫອມ
dipping sauces	jaew	ແຈ່ວ
dried shrimp	kûng hàeng	ກຸ້ງແຫ້ງ
fish sauce	nâm pạa	ນ້ຳປາ
fish sauce with chillies	nâm pạa sai màak phét	ນ້ຳປາໃສ່ ໝາກເຜັດ
ginger	khǐing	ຂີງ
ground peanuts	thua dịn	ຖົ່ວດິນ
lemongrass	hǔa sǒng khái	ຫົວສິງໄຄ
lime juice	nâm màak náo	ນ້ຳໝາກນາວ
salt	kẹua	ເກືອ
sesame	màak ngáa	ໝາກງາ
soy sauce	nâm sá-ǐu	ນ້ຳສະອີ້ວ
sugar	nâm-tạan	ນ້ຳຕານ
sweet basil	bại hǒh-la-pháa	ໃບໂຫລະພາ
tamarind	màak khǎam	ໝາກຂາມ
vinegar	nâm sòm	ນ້ຳສົ້ມ

COOKING METHODS — ວິທີປຸງແຕ່ງອາຫານ

óp — ອົບ
 baked

tôm — ຕົ້ມ
 boiled

súk — ສຸກ
 cooked/ripe

kąeng — ແກງ
 curried

jęun — ຈືນ
 fried in large pieces

khùa phák thíam phik thái — ຂົ້ວຜັກທຽມພິກໄທ
 fried with garlic and black pepper

khùa khǐing — ຂົ້ວຂີງ
 fried with ginger

pîing — ປີ້ງ
 grilled, barbecued or roasted

díp — ດິບ
 raw/unripe

nèung — ໜື້ງ
 steamed (fish, rice only)

khùa (phát) — ຂົ້ວ (ຜັດ)
 stir-fried or fried in small pieces

FRUIT — ໝາກໄມ້

apple (usually imported, year-round)
 màak pǫhm — ໝາກໂປມ

banana (year-round)
 màak kûay — ໝາກກ້ວຍ

mandarin orange (year-round)
 màak kîang — ໝາກກ້ຽງ

watermelon (year-round)
 màak móh — ໝາກໂມ

TROPICAL DELIGHTS

Laos, like its South-East Asian neighbours, offers travellers an opportunity to indulge in a wide range of tropical fruit – don't miss out!

ໝາກພ້າວ — màak phâo

coconut – grated for cooking when mature, eaten with a spoon when young; juice is sweetest in young coconuts (year-round)

ໝາກຂຽບ — màak khìap

custard-apple (July to October)

ທຸລຽນ — thu-lían

durian – held in high esteem by South-East Asians, but most Westerners dislike this fruit. There are several varieties and seasons, so keep trying.

ໝາກສີດາ — màak sĭi-dạa

guava (year-round)

ໝາກມີ້ — màak mîi

jackfruit – similar in outward appearance to durian but much easier to take (year round)

ໝາກນາວ — màak náo

lime (year-round)

ໝາກຍຳໄຍ — màak nyám nyái

longan – 'dragon's eyes', small, brown, spherical, similar to rambutan (July to October)

ໝາກລິ້ນຈີ່ màak lîn-jii
lychee (July to October)

ໝາກມ່ວງ màak muang
mango – several varieties and seasons

ໝາກມັງຄຸດ màak máng-khut
mangosteen – round, purple fruit with juicy white flesh (April to September)

ໝາກນັດ màak nat
pineapple (year-round)

ໝາກຫຸ່ງ màak hung
papaya (year-round)

ໝາກເງາະ màak ngaw
rambutan – red, hairy-skinned fruit with grape-like interior (July to September)

ໝາກກຽງ màak kịang
rose-apple – small, apple-like texture, very fragrant (April to July)

ອ້ອຍ âwy
sugarcane (year round)

ໝາກຂາມ màak khăam
tamarind – comes in sweet as well as tart varieties (year-round)

SWEETS ເຂືອງຫວານ

Restaurant menus rarely offer Lao sweets (ເຂືອງຫວານ, kheuang wăan). Instead the Lao buy these fresh in local morning markets or from street vendors in the evening. Typical ingredients include sticky rice, rice flour, palm and cane sugar, agar-agar (gelatin made from a type of seaweed), shredded coconut, coconut extract, egg yolks and various kinds of fruit.

banana in coconut milk
nâm wăan màak kûay ນ້ຳຫວານໝາກກ້ວຍ

cakes made with sticky rice flour
khào nŏm ເຂົ້າໜົມ

custard
khào săng-kha-nyăa ສັງຂະຫຍາ

egg custard
khào-nŏm màw kạeng ເຂົ້າໜົມໝໍ້ແກງ

red sticky rice in coconut cream
khào nĭaw dạeng ເຂົ້າໜຽວແດງ

sticky rice in coconut cream and ripe mango
khào nĭaw màak muang ເຂົ້າໜຽວໝາກມ່ວງ

sticky rice in coconut milk cooked in bamboo
khào lăam ເຂົ້າຫລາມ

sweetened sticky rice steamed in banana leaves
khào tôm ເຂົ້າຕົ້ມ

DRINKS – NON-ALCOHOLIC
ດື່ມ-ເຄື່ອງດື່ມທີ່ບໍ່ມີທາດເຫຼົ້າ

Water
ນ້ຳ

Drinking water (ນ້ຳດື່ມ, **nâm deum**) is purified for drinking purposes, whether boiled or otherwise treated. All water offered to customers in restaurants or hotels will be purified, so one needn't fret about the safety of taking a sip from a proffered glass or pitcher. In restaurants and most foodstalls, you can order **nâm deum** by the bottle, or you can ask for drinking water by the glass at no charge. The latter is usually drawn from 20L bottles of purified water or water boiled by the proprietors for drinking purposes.

boiled water	**nâm tôm**	ນ້ຳຕົ້ມ
drinking water	**nâm deum**	ນ້ຳດື່ມ
ice	**nâm kâwn**	ນ້ຳກ້ອນ

Coffee & Tea ກາເຟແລະນ້ຳຊາ

Good coffee is grown in the Bolaven Plateau area of Southern Laos. The Lao tend to brew coffee using pure coffee beans (rarely adding ground peanuts or chicory as in Thailand). Traditionally Lao coffee is roasted by wholesalers, ground by vendors and filtered just before serving. The typical Lao restaurant – especially those in hotels, guesthouses and other tourist-oriented establishments – serves instant coffee with packets of artificial, non-dairy creamer on the side.

If you want real Lao coffee ask for **kạa-féh thŏng** (ກາເຟຖົງ, bag coffee), or **kạ-féh tôm** (ກາເຟຕົ້ມ, boiled coffee), prepared by pouring hot water through a bag-shaped cloth filter containing ground coffee.

The Lao usually serve filtered coffee mixed with sugar. Some shops also add sweetened condensed milk. If you don't want sugar or milk, ask for **kạa-féh dạm** (ກາເຟດຳ, black coffee) and **baw sai nâm-tạan** (ບໍ່ໃສ່ນ້ຳຕານ, without sugar). Lao coffee usually comes in a small glass instead of a ceramic cup. Grasp the hot glass along the rim to avoid burnt fingers.

In Central and Southern Laos, coffee is almost always served with a chaser of hot **nâm sáa** (ນ້ຳຊາ, weak tea), while in the north it's typically served with a glass of plain hot water.

Chinese-style (green or semi-cured) teas predominate in Chinese and Vietnamese restaurants and are always served plain, ie, without sugar or milk. Black, Indian-style tea is typically found only in restaurants or foodstalls that serve Lao coffee. If you order **sáa hâwn** (ຊາຮ້ອນ, hot tea), it may arrive with sugar and condensed milk, so be sure to specify **sáa dạm baw sai nâm-tạan** (ຊາດຳບໍ່ໃສ່ນ້ຳຕານ) if you prefer black tea without milk and/or sugar.

hot water	nâm hâwn	ນ້ຳຮ້ອນ
cold water	nâm yén	ນ້ຳເຢັນ
hot Lao coffee with milk and sugar	kạa-féh nóm hâwn	ກາເຟນົມຮ້ອນ
hot Lao coffee with sugar, no milk	kạa-féh dạm	ກາເຟດຳ
hot Nescafé with milk and sugar	naet nóm	ແນດນົມ
hot Nescafé with sugar, no milk	naet dạm	ແນດດຳ
iced Lao coffee with sugar, no milk	kạa-féh nóm yén	ກາເຟນົມເຢັນ
iced Lao coffee with milk and sugar	òh-lîang	ໂອລ້ຽງ
weak tea	nâm sáa	ນ້ຳຊາ
hot Lao tea with sugar	sáa hâwn	ຊາຮ້ອນ
hot Lao tea with milk and sugar	sáa nóm hâwn	ຊານົມຮ້ອນ
iced Lao tea with milk and sugar	sáa nóm yén	ຊານົມເຢັນ
iced Lao tea with sugar, no milk	sáa wăan yén	ຊາຫວານເຢັນ
no sugar	baw sai nâm-tạan	ບໍ່ໃສ່ນ້ຳຕານ
Ovaltine	oh-wan-tin	ໂອວັນຕິນ
orange juice (or orange soda)	nâm màak kîang	ນ້ຳໝາກກ້ຽງ
plain milk	nâm nóm	ນ້ຳນົມ
yogurt	nóm sòm	ນົມສົ້ມ

FOOD

DRINKS – ALCOHOLIC ດື່ມ-ເຫຼົ້າ

Beer ເບຍ

Several kinds of beer are brewed by the Lao Brewery Company on the outskirts of Vientiane. Least expensive but very drinkable is LBC's draft beer (ເບຍສົດ, bịa sòt), which is only available in beer bars in Vientiane. LBC also bottles a Bia Lao (the French label reads Bière Larue) – look for the tiger's head on the label. In the northern provinces bordering China, various Chinese brands of beer are available – these generally cost less than Lao beer.

Distilled Spirits ເຫຼົ້າ

Rice whisky or **lào láo** (ເຫຼົ້າລາວ, Lao liquor) is a popular drink among lowland Lao. The government produces several brands which are very similar in taste to Thailand's famous 'Mekong whisky' and are best taken over ice with a splash of soda and a squeeze of lime.

In rural provinces, a weaker version of **lào láo** is fermented by households or villages. Strictly speaking, it's not legal but no-one seems to care. It's not always safe to drink, however, since unboiled water is often added during and after the fermentation process.

beer	bịa	ເບຍ
draught beer	bịa sót	ເບຍສົດ
Lao rice whisky	lào láo	ເຫຼົ້າລາວ
soda water	nâm sŏh-dạa	ນ້ຳໂສດາ
glass	jàwk	ຈອກ
bottle	kâew	ແກ້ວ

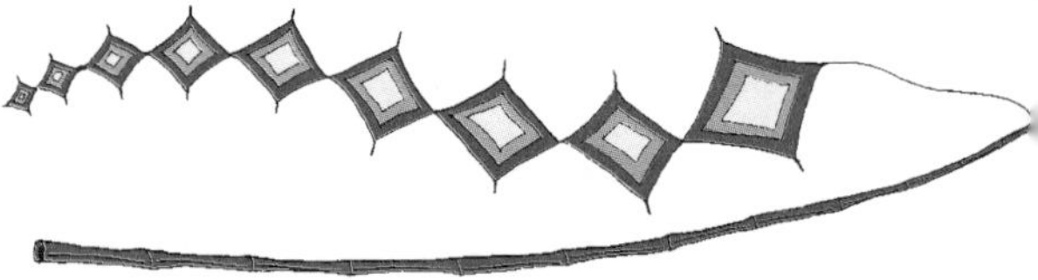

WEATHER ອາກາດ

How's the weather?
ąa-káat pęn jang-dąi — ອາກາດເປັນຈັ່ງໃດ
The weather is nice today.
mêu-nîi ąa-kàat dįi — ມື້ນີ້ອາກາດດີ
The weather isn't good.
ąa-kàat baw dįi — ອາກາດບໍ່ດີ
Is it going to rain?
fŏn sii tók lĕu baw — ຝົນຊິຕົກຫລືບໍ່

It's ...

windy	lóm phat	ລົມພັດ
not windy	lóm baw phat	ລົມບໍ່ພັດ
very cold	năo lăai	ໜາວຫລາຍ
very hot	hâwn lăai	ຮ້ອນຫລາຍ
raining hard	fŏn tók nak	ຝົນຕົກໜັກ
flooding	nám thûam	ນ້ຳຖ້ວມ

cool weather	ąa-kàat yęn	ອາກາດເຢັນ
hot weather	ąa-kàat hâwn	ອາກາດຮ້ອນ
fog	nâm màwk	ນ້ຳໝອກ
lightning	fâa mâep	ຟ້າແມບ
monsoon	máw-la-sŭm	ມໍລະສຸມ
weather	ąa-kàat	ອາກາດ

TREKKING ການເດີນປ່າ

Are there guided treks?
míi pha-nak-ngáan nám thiaw baw dǫen paa — ມີພະນັກງານ ນຳທ່ຽວບໍ່ເດີນປ່າ
Do we need a guide?
jąm pęn tâwng míi pha-nak-ngáan nám thiaw baw — ຈຳເປັນຕ້ອງມີ ພະນັກງານ ນຳທ່ຽວບໍ່

Does the price include ...?	láa-kháa huam nám khaa ... baw	ລາຄາຮ່ວມ ນຳຄ່າ ... ບໍ່
food	ąa-hăan	ອາຫານ
transport	khŏn-song	ຂົນສົ່ງ

How many hours per day will we walk?
já nyaang mêu-la ják sua-móhng — ຈະຍ່າງມື້ລະຈັກ ຊົ່ວໂມງ

Is it a difficult walk?
tháang pąi nyâak baw — ທາງໄປຫຍາກບໍ່

I/We would like to hire a guide.
yàak jâang pha-nak-ngáan nám thiaw — ຢາກຈ້າງ ພະນັກງານນຳທ່ຽວ

backpack	bąa-lóh/thŏng pêh	ບາໂລ/ຖົງເປ້
compass	khĕm thit	ເຂັມທິດ
first-aid kit	thŏng yáa pá-jąam bąan	ຖົງຢາປະຈັນບ້ານ
guide (person)	pha-nak-ngáan nám thiaw	ພະນັກງານ ນຳທ່ຽວ
guided trek	pha-nak ngáan nám thiaw dọen paa	ພະນັກງານນຳ ທ່ຽວເດີນປ່າ
hiking boots	kòep dọen paa	ເກີບເດີນປ່າ
map	phăen-thii	ແຜນທີ່
mountain climbing	kąan pįin phúu	ການປີນພູ
provisions	kheuang dọen paa	ເຄື່ອງເດີນປ່າ
rope	sêuak	ເຊືອກ
signpost	pâai bàwk tháang	ປ້າຍບອກທາງ
tour/trek	thawng thiaw; dọen paa	ທ່ອງທ່ຽວ/ເດີນປ່າ
to walk	nyaang	ຍ່າງ

Where is the trail to ...?
tháang pąi ... yuu săi — ທາງໄປ ... ຢູ່ໃສ

Which is the shortest route?
tháang dąi sàn kwaa — ທາງໃດສັ້ນກວ່າ

Which is the easiest route?
tháang dąi sá-dùak kwaa — ທາງໃດສະດວກກ່ວາ

IN THE COUNTRY

Where's the nearest village?
muu bâan thii yuu kâi kwaa muu săi — ໝູ່ບ້ານທີ່ຢູ່ໃກ້ກ່ວາໝູ່ຢູ່ໃສ

Is it safe to climb this mountain?
khêun phuu nîi pàwt phái baw — ຂຶ້ນພູນີ້ປອດໄພບໍ່

Is there a hut up there?
yuu thóeng phúu míi thĭang hai baw — ຢູ່ເທິງພູມີຖຽງໄຮ່ບໍ່

I'd like to talk to someone who knows this area.
yàak lóm káp phûu hûu phêun thii nîi — ຢາກລົມກັບຜູ້ຮູ້ພື້ນທີ່ນີ້

How far is it from ... to ...?
tae ... thŏeng ... kại thao dại — ແຕ່ ... ເຖິງ ... ໄກເທົ່າໃດ

Where have you come from?
jâo máa tae săi — ເຈົ້າມາແຕ່ໃສ

How long did it take you?
jâo sâi wéh-láa lăai pạan dại — ເຈົ້າໃຊ້ເວລາຫລາຍປານໃດ

How many ...?	ják ...	ຈັກ ...
days	mêu	ມື້
hours	sua-móhng	ຊົ່ວໂມງ
kilometres	kí-lóh-maet	ກິໂລແມັດ
metres	maet	ແມັດ

DID YOU KNOW ...

From its source on the Tibetan Plateau, the Mekong River passes through Yunnan, then into Laos and Thailand, dropping by Cambodia before entering the South China Sea through its delta in Vietnam – it is the 12th longest river in the world.

IN THE COUNTRY

I'm lost.
khàwy lŏng tháang — ຂ້ອຍຫລົງທາງ

Does this path go to ...?
tháang nîi pại hâwt ... — ທາງນີ້ໄປຮອດ ...

How long is the trail?
tháang nyáo pạan dại — ທາງຍາວປານໃດ

Is the track well-marked?
míi pâai bàwk tháang baw — ມີປ້າຍບອກທາງບໍ່

Can we go through here?
phaan tháang nîi dâi baw — ຜ່ານທາງນີ້ໄດ້ບໍ່

When does it get dark?
ják móhng sii mêut — ຈັກໂມງຊິມືດ

Where can we buy supplies?
sêu kheuang sâi dâi yuu săi — ຊື້ເຄື່ອງໃຊ້ໄດ້ຢູ່ໃສ

Who lives here?
phăi yuu bawn nîi — ໃຜຢູ່ບ່ອນນີ້

Can I/we stay in this village?
khàwy/phŭak háo phak yuu bâan nîi dâi baw — ຂ້ອຍ/ພວກເຮົາພັກຢູ່ບ້ານນີ້ໄດ້ບໍ່

Can I/we sleep here?
khàwy/phŭak háo náwn yuu nîi dâi baw — ຂ້ອຍ/ພວກເຮົານອນຢູ່ນີ້ໄດ້ບໍ່

blanket	phàa hom	ຜ້າຫົ່ມ
hill tribe (High Lao)	sáo khăo	ຊາວເຂົາ
lodging	bawn phak	ບ່ອນພັກ
medicine	yạa	ຢາ
mosquitoes	nyúng	ຍຸງ
mosquito coil	yạa jút kạn nyúng	ຢາຈຸດກັນຍຸງ
mosquito net	mûng	ມຸ້ງ
opium	yạa fin	ຢາຝິ່ນ
raft	pháe	ແພ
village headman	nai bâan	ນາຍບ້ານ
water	nâm	ນ້ຳ

CAMPING ການຕັ້ງຄ້າຍ

In general, the Lao government permits foreigners to camp outdoors only when they are participating in a tour led by a Lao PDR-licensed tour agency. This may change as Laos opens further to tourism.

camping	kąan tâng khêm	ການຕັ້ງເຄັ້ມ
campsite	bawn tâng khêm	ບ່ອນຕັ້ງເຄັ້ມ
rope	sêuak	ເຊືອກ
sleeping bag	thŏng náwn	ຖົງນອນ
tent	tùup phàa	ຕູບຜ້າ
torch (flashlight)	fái săai	ໄຟສາຍ

Is there a campsite nearby?
yuu kâi nîi míi bawn tâng khêm baw — ຢູ່ໃກ້ນີ້ມີບ່ອນຕັ້ງເຄັ້ມບໍ່

Where's the nearest campsite?
bawn tâng khêm thii kâi thii sút yuu săi — ບ່ອນຕັ້ງເຄັ້ມທີ່ໃກ້ ທີ່ສຸດຢູ່ໃສ

Is drinking water available?
míi nâm deum baw — ມີນ້ຳດື່ມບໍ່

Can I/we put a tent here?
[khàwy; phûak háo] táng tùup phàa yuu nîi dâi baw — ຂ້ອຍ; ພວກເຮົາ ຕັ້ງ ຕູບຜ້າຢູ່ນີ້ໄດ້ບໍ່

Is it safe?
pàwt phái baw — ປອດໄພບໍ່

Is drinking water available?
míi nâm deum baw — ມີນ້ຳດື່ມບໍ່

CYCLING ການຂີ່ລົດຖີບ

Bicycles are a popular form of transport throughout urban Laos and can be hired cheaply almost anywhere there are guesthouses. These Thai- or Chinese-made street bikes come in varying degrees of usability, so be sure to inspect the bikes thoroughly before renting. Lao customs doesn't object to visitors bringing bicycles into the country.

Where can I hire a bike?
khàwy já sao lot thìip dâi yuu săi — ຂ້ອຍຈະເຊົ່າລົດຖີບໄດ້ຢູ່ໃສ

How much is it for ...?	khaa sao thao dạai taw ...	ຄ່າເຊົ່າເທົ່າໃດຕໍ່ ...
an hour	neung sua-móhng	ໜຶ່ງຊົ່ວໂມງ
the morning	tạwn sâo	ຕອນເຊົ້າ
the afternoon	tạwn baai	ຕອນບ່າຍ
the day	neung wan	ໜຶ່ງວັນ

Where can I find second-hand bikes for sale?
míi lot thìip méu săwng khăai yuu săi — ມີລົດຖີບມືສອງຂາຍຢູ່ໃສ

Is it within cycling distance?
tháang nîi pẹn wóng jạwn săm-láp khii lot thìip baw — ທາງນີ້ເປັນວົງຈອນສໍາລັບຂີ່ລົດຖີບບໍ່

Is the trail suitable for bikes?
tháang nîi máw săm-láp khii lot thìip baw — ທາງນີ້ເໝາະສໍາລັບຂີ່ລົດຖີບບໍ່

I have a flat tyre.
tịin lot khàwy hua — ຕີນລົດຂ້ອຍຮົ່ວ

bicycle	lot thìip	ລົດຖີບ
brakes	hàam	ຫ້າມ
to cycle	thìip	ຖີບ
gear stick	khan kịa	ຄັນເກຍ

handlebars	khǎo	ເຂົາ
helmet	mùak kạn nawk	ໝວກກັນນ໊ອກ
inner tube	yáang nái	ຢາງໃນ
lights	fái tạa	ໄຟຕາ
padlock	ká-jạe	ກະແຈ
pump	kâwng sùup	ກ້ອງສູບ
puncture	hua	ຮົ່ວ
saddle	ạan	ອານ
wheel	kọng lot	ກົງລົດ

GEOGRAPHY ພູມີສາດ

Many town and village names in Laos incorporate the following geographic or demographic features.

Ban or Baan (village)	bâan	ບ້ານ
Don (river island)	dạwn	ດອນ
Khok or Kok (knoll or mound)	khôhk	ໂຄກ
Muang (city or district)	méuang	ເມືອງ
Nakhon (large city)	na-kháwn	ນະຄອນ
Nam (river in Northern Laos)	nâm	ນ້ຳ
Non (hill, knoll or mound)	nóhn	ໂນນ
Nong (pond/lake)	nǎwng	ໜອງ
Pak (mouth – usually at a river mouth)	pàak	ປາກ
Se (rivers in Southern Laos)	séh	ເຊ
Vieng (city)	wíang	ວຽງ
Xieng (city)	síang	ຊຽງ

A POTTED HISTORY

PLAIN OF JARS
ທົ່ງໄຫຫີນ

Among the most enigmatic sights in Laos are several meadow-like areas in Xieng Khuang Province littered with large stone jars. Quite a few theories have been advanced as to the functions of the stone jars – that they were used as sarcophagi, as wine fermenters or for rice storage – but the most likely theory suggests they held relics associated with ritual reburial. White quartzite rocks have also been found lying next to some of the jars, along with vases that may have contained human remains.

Aerial photographic evidence suggests that a thin 'track' of jars may link the various jar sites in Xieng Khuang, and some researchers hope future excavations will uncover sealed jars whose contents may be relatively intact.

The jars are commonly said to be 2000 years old, but in the absence of any organic material associated with the jars – eg, bones or food remains – there's no reliable way to date them. The jars may be associated with the equally mysterious stone megaliths found off Route 6 on the way north to Sam Neua, and/or with large Dongson drum-shaped stone objects discovered in Luang Prabang Province. All of the unanswered questions regarding the Plain of Jars (thong hăi hĭn) make this area ripe for archaeological investigation, a proceeding that has been slowed by years of war and by the presence of UXO (unexploded ordnance).

Site 1, 15km south-west of Phonsavan and the largest of the various sites, features 250 jars which weigh from 600kg to one tonne each; the biggest of them weighs as much as six tonnes. The jars have been fashioned from solid stone, most from a tertiary conglomerate known as molasses, akin to sandstone, and a few from granite.

GEOGRAPHIC FEATURES ພູມມີປະເທດອື່ນ

cave	thàm	ຖ້ຳ
cliff	phăa	ຜາ
countryside	bâan nâwk	ບ້ານນອກ
field (dry)	hai	ໄຮ່
footpath	tháang nyaang	ທາງຍ່າງ
forest	paa	ປ່າ
hill	phúu nâwy	ພູນ້ອຍ
jungle	dọng	ດົງ
mountain	phúu khăo	ພູເຂົາ
mountain peak	jạwm phúu	ຈອມພູ
nature	thám-ma-sâat	ທຳມະຊາດ
rice field (wet)	náa	ນາ
river	nâm	ນ້ຳ
riverbank	fang nâm	ຝັ່ງນ້ຳ
river rapids	kâeng	ແກ້ງ
sea	tha-léh	ທະເລ
spring/well	baw nâm	ບໍ່ນ້ຳ
stone	hĭn	ຫີນ
stream	hùay	ຫ້ວຍ
swamp	bẹung	ບຶງ
trail	tháang thiaw	ທາງທ່ຽວ
waterfall	nâm tók tàat	ນ້ຳຕົກຕາດ

ANIMALS ສັດປ່າ

ant	mót	ໝົດ
banteng (type of wild cattle)	ngúa dàeng	ງົວແດງ
barking deer	fáan	ຟານ
bear	mĭi	ໝີ
bee	mae phòeng	ແມ່ເຜິ້ງ
bird	nok	ນົກ
butterfly	máeng ká-bêua	ແມງກະເບື້ອ

civet	ngĭan	ເຫງັນ
cockroach	máeng sàap	ແມງສາບ
cow	ngúa	ງົວ
crocodile	khàe	ແຂ້
deer	kwạang	ກວາງ
dog	măa	ໝາ
dolphin	pạa lóh-máa	ປາໂລມາ
duck	pét	ເປັດ
elephant	sâang	ຊ້າງ
fish	pạa	ປາ
fishing cat	sĕua pạa	ເສືອປາ
fly	máeng wán	ແມງວັນ
frog	kóp	ກົບ
gaur	ká-thíng	ກະທິງ
gecko	káp-kâe	ກັບແກ້
gibbon	sa-níi	ຊະນີ
horse	mâa	ມ້າ
leaf monkey	khaang	ຄ່າງ
leopard	sĕua dạo	ເສືອດາວ
monkey	líng	ລິງ
rabbit	ká-tại	ກະຕ່າຍ
rhinoceros	hâet	ແຮດ
scorpion	máeng ngáo	ແມງເງົາ
shrimp	kûng	ກຸ້ງ
snake	ngúu	ງູ
snake (venomous)	ngúu phít	ງູພິດ
tiger	sĕua khong	ເສືອໂຄ່ງ
turtle	tao	ເຕົ່າ
water buffalo	khu-wáai	ຄວາຍ
water fowl	nok nâm	ນົກນ້ຳ
wild animals	sát paa	ສັດປ່າ
wild buffalo	khuáai paa	ຄວາຍປ່າ
young animal; offspring	lûuk sát	ລູກສັດ

ຕົ້ນ

PLANTS

bamboo	phai	ໄຜ່
dipterocarp	yáang	ຍາງ
flower	dàwk mâi	ດອກໄມ້
grass/herb	nyàa	ຫຍ້າ
pine	tôn sŏn	ຕົ້ນສົນ
tree	tôn mâi	ຕົ້ນໄມ້
teak	tôn sák	ຕົ້ນສັກ

DID YOU KNOW ...

The *dipterocarp* is a member of a family of evergreen trees commonly found in south Asia and Africa, named for its helicopter-like seed pods. It's generally a large tree, known for its leathery leaves and aromatic resins. The tree can be used as a source of timber and in the production of varnishes and herbal remedies.

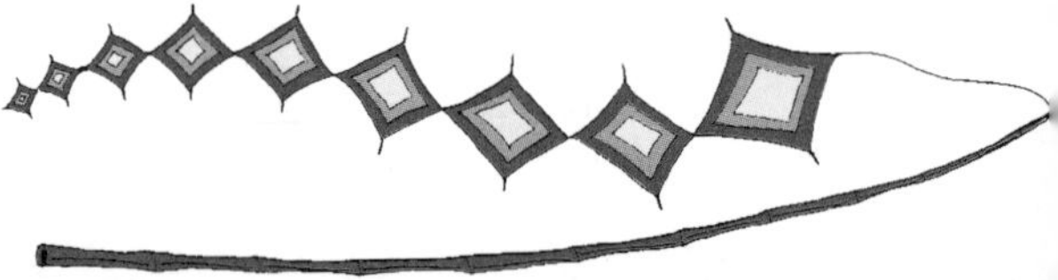

ສຸຂະພາບ HEALTH

I need a ...	khàwy tâwng-kạan ...	ຂ້ອຍຕ້ອງການ ...
dentist	mǎw pụa khàew	ໝໍປົວແຂ້ວ
doctor	thaan mǎw	ທ່ານໝໍ
Where's the nearest ...?	... yùu sǎi	... ຢູ່ໃສ
chemist	khóm bụng yáa	ຄົມບຸງຢາ
hospital	hóhng mǎw	ໂຮງໝໍ

I'm sick.
khàwy baw sá-bạai ຂ້ອຍບໍ່ສະບາຍ

My friend is sick.
pheuan khàwy baw sá-bạai ເພື່ອນຂ້ອຍບໍ່ສະບາຍ

I need a doctor who speaks English.
khàwy tâwng-kạan thaan mǎw hûu pháa-sǎa ạng-kít ຂ້ອຍຕ້ອງການທ່ານ ໝໍຮູ້ພາສາອັງກິດ

Could the doctor come here?
thaan mǎw máa nîi dâi baw ທ່ານໝໍມານີ້ໄດ້ບໍ່

WOMEN'S HEALTH ສຸຂະພາບແມ່ຍິງ

Could I see a female doctor?
khàwy khǎw phop thaan mǎw phùu nyíng dâi baw ຂ້ອຍຂໍພົບທ່ານ ໝໍຜູ້ຍິງໄດ້ບໍ່

I'm pregnant.
khàwy thěu pháa-máan ຂ້ອຍຖືພາມານ

I'm on the Pill.
khàwy kịn yáa khúm ຂ້ອຍກິນຢາຄຸມ

I haven't had my period for ... weeks.
pá-jạm dẹuan khàwy baw máa dâi ... ạa-thit lâew ປະຈຳເດືອນຂ້ອຍບໍ່ ມາໄດ້ ... ອາທິດແລ້ວ

AILMENTS ການເຈັບເປັນ

I'm tired.	khàwy meuay	ຂ້ອຍເໝື່ອຍ
I'm not well.	khàwy baw sá-bạai	ຂ້ອຍບໍ່ສະບາຍ
I have a cold.	pẹn wát	ເປັນຫວັດ
I have a fever.	pẹn khài	ເປັນໄຂ້
My stomach aches.	pùat thâwng	ປວດທ້ອງ
I have diarrhoea.	lóng thâwng	ລົງທ້ອງ
It hurts here.	jép yuu nîi	ເຈັບຢູ່ນີ້
I can't sleep.	náwn baw lap	ນອນບໍ່ລັບ
My head aches.	pùat hŭa	ປວດຫົວ
My back hurts.	pùat lăng	ປວດຫລັງ

There's pain in my chest.
jép nàa óek ເຈັບໜ້າເອິກ

I have a sore throat.
jép kháw ເຈັບຄໍ

I have vomited several times.
hàak lăai theua ຮາກຫລາຍເທື່ອ

I have been like this for two weeks.
pẹn naew nîi dai săwng ເປັນແນວນີ້ໄດ້ສອງ
ạa-thit lâew ອາທິດແລ້ວ

Is it serious?
pẹn nák baw ເປັນໜັກບໍ່

I feel ...	khàwy hûu-séuk ...	ຂ້ອຍຮູ້ສຶກ ...
dizzy	ịn hụa	ວິນຫົວ
shivery	năo son	ໜາວສັ່ນ
weak	awn phía	ອ່ອນເພຍ

ache	pùat	ປວດ
AIDS	lôhk èht	ໂລກເອດສ
allergy	phâe	ແພ້
anaemia	lôhk lêuat jạang	ໂລກເລືອດຈາງ
asthma	lôhk hèut	ໂລກຫືດ
blister	pẹn tum	ເປັນຕຸ່ມ

HEALTH

bronchitis	làwt lóm ák-sèhp	ຫລອດລົມອັກເສບ
burn	fái mâi	ໄຟໄໝ້
cancer	ma-léhng	ມະເລງ
cholera	a-hí-wáa	ອະຫິວາ
cough	ại	ໄອ
cramps	pân (phùuk)	ປັ້ນ (ຜູກ)
dengue fever	khài lêuat àwk	ໄຂ້ເລືອດອອກ
diabetes	lôhk bạo wǎan	ໂລກເບົາຫວານ
diarrhoea	lóng thâwng	ລົງທ້ອງ
dysentery	lôhk thâwng bít	ໂລກທ້ອງບິດ
fever	khài	ໄຂ້
headache	pùat hǔa	ປວດຫົວ
heart condition	sá-phâap hǔa jại	ສະພາບຫົວໃຈ
hepatitis	tàp ák-sèhp	ຕັບອັກເສບ
infection	séum sêua	ຊຶມເຊື້ອ

inflammation	ák-sèhp	ອັກເສບ
influenza	khài wát nyai	ໄຂ້ຫວັດໃຫຍ່
lice	tọh hǎo	ໂຕເຫົາ
malaria	khài yúng	ໄຂ້ຍຸງ
migraine	jep hǔa háeng	ເຈັບຫົວແຮງ
pneumonia	lôhk pàwt bụam	ໂລກປອດບວມ
rabies	lôhk pẹn wâw	ໂລກເປັນວໍ້
rash	tum	ຕຸ່ມ
sore throat	jep kháw	ເຈັບຄໍ
sprain	pùat khat	ປວດຂັດ
stomachache	pùat thâwng	ປວດທ້ອງ
sunburn	mâi dàet	ໄໝ້ແດດ
toothache	jép khàew	ເຈັບແຂ້ວ
veneral disease	kạm-ma lôhk	ກາມະໂລກ

THEY MAY SAY ...

pẹn nyăng — ເປັນຫຍັງ
What's the matter?

jâo jép nyăng baw — ເຈົ້າເຈັບຫຍັງບໍ່
Do you feel any pain?

jép yuu săi — ເຈັບຢູ່ໃສ
Where does it hurt?

pẹn bàep nîi dọn bạan-dại lâew — ເປັນແບບນີ້ດົນປານໃດແລ້ວ
How long have you been like this?

jâo khóei pẹn băep nîi baw — ເຈົ້າເຄີຍເປັນແບບນີ້ບໍ່
Have you had this before?

jâo kịn yáa baw — ເຈົ້າກິນຢາບໍ່
Are you on medication?

jâo phâe ạn-dại baw — ເຈົ້າແພ້ອັນໃດບໍ່
Are you allergic to anything?

jâo thĕu pháa-máan baw — ເຈົ້າຖືພາມານບໍ່
Are you pregnant?

PARTS OF THE BODY ພາກສ່ວນຂອງຮ່າງກາຍ

arm	khăen	ແຂນ
back	lăng	ຫລັງ
breast	tâo nóm	ເຕົ້ານົມ
chest	óek	ເອິກ
ear	hŭu	ຫູ
eye	tạa	ຕາ
face	nàa	ໜ້າ
finger	nîu méu	ນິ້ວມື
foot/feet	tịin	ຕີນ
hand	méu	ມື
head	hŭa	ຫົວ
heart	hŭa jại	ຫົວໃຈ
jaw	kháang ká-tại	ຄາງກະໄຕ

kidney	màak khai lăng	ໝາກໄຂ່ຫລັງ
knee	hŭa khao	ຫົວເຂົ່າ
leg	khăa	ຂາ
liver	táp	ຕັບ
lungs	pàwt	ປອດ
mouth	pàak	ປາກ
muscle	kâam sîin	ກ້າມຊີ້ນ
nose	dạng	ດັງ
penis	a-wái-ya-wa	ອະໄວຍະວະ
	phêht sáai	ເພດຊາຍ
ribs	ká-dùuk khàang	ກະດູກຂ້າງ
shoulders	baa-lai	ບ່າໄລ່
spine	ká-dùuk săn lăng	ກະດູກສັນຫລັງ
stomach	thâwng (ká-phaw)	ທ້ອງ (ກະເພາະ)
testicles	ạn-tha (hăm)	ອັນທະ (ຫຳ)
throat	kháw	ຄໍ
toe	nîu tịin	ນິ້ວຕີນ
tooth/teeth	khàew	ແຂ້ວ
vagina	sâwng khâwt	ຊ່ອງຄອດ

AT THE CHEMIST ຢູ່ຮ້ານຂາຍຢາ

antibiotics	yáa tâan sêua (sa-nit kịn)	ຢາຕ້ານເຊື້ອ (ຊະນິດກິນ)
antiseptic	yáa tâan sêua (sa-nit tháa)	ຢາຕ້ານເຊື້ອ (ຊະນິດທາ)
aspirin	àet-sá-pẹh-lín	ແອສເປລິນ
Band-Aid (plaster)	phàa tít bàat	ຜ້າຕິດບາດ
bandage	phàa haw bàat	ຜ້າຫໍ່ບາດ
condom (latex)	thŏng yạang á-náa-mái	ຖົງຢາງອະນາໄມ
gauze	phàa kâw	ຜ້າກໍ້
injection	sák yạa	ສັກຢາ
insulin	yạa kâe lôhk	ຢາແກ້ໂລກ
	bạo wăan	ເບົາຫວານ

morphine	máw-fíin	ມໍຟີນ
painkiller	yạa kâe pùat	ຢາແກ້ປວດ
pill/tablet	yạ met	ຢາເມັດ
prescription	bại sang yạa	ໃບສັ່ງຢາ
sleeping medication	yạa náwn láp	ຢານອນລັບ
vitamin	wi-tạa-mín	ວິຕາມິນ

I need something for ...
khàwy tâwng-kạan ạn-dại ạn neung pheua ...
ຂ້ອຍຕ້ອງການອັນໃດອັນໜຶ່ງເພື່ອ ...

I have a prescription.
khàwy míi bại sang yáa
ຂ້ອຍມີໃບສັ່ງຢາ

How many times a day?
mêu-la ják theua
ມື້ລະຈັກເທື່ອ

(Four) times a day.
mêu-la (sii) theua
ມື້ລະ (ສີ່) ເທື່ອ

How much per tablet/pill?
láa kháa met-la thao dại
ລາຄາເມັດລະເທົ່າໃດ

Useful Words

ຄຳສັບທີ່ເປັນປະໂຫຍດ

accident	ú-bát-tí-hèht	ອຸບັດຕິເຫດ
addict	khón tít yạa	ຄົນຕິດຢາ
allergic (to)	phâe	ແພ້
ambulance	lot hóhng mǎw	ລົດໂຮງໝໍ
bite	kát	ກັດ
blood test	kùat lêuat	ກວດເລືອດ
blood	lêuat	ເລືອດ
bone	ká-dùuk	ກະດູກ
faint	pẹn lóm	ເປັນລົມ
hospital	hóhng mǎw	ໂຮງໝໍ
ill	puay	ປ່ວຍ
inject	sák yáa	ສັກຢາ

HEALTH

itch	khán	ຄັນ
mentally ill	sĭa jít	ເສຍຈິດ
nurse	náang pha-yáa-bạan	ນາງພະຍາບານ
pain	khwáam jép-pùat	ຄວາມເຈັບປວດ
patient (n)	khón jép	ຄົນເຈັບ
pharmacy	hâan khăai yạa	ຮ້ານຂາຍຢາ
pregnant	thĕu pháa-máan	ຖືພາມານ
skin	phĭu năng	ຜິວໜັງ
vitamins	wi-tạa-mín	ວິຕາມິນ
wound	bàat phăe (baat jép)	ບາດແຜ (ບາດເຈັບ)

I feel better/worse.
khàwy hûu-séuk dị khêun/ jép-kwaa kao
ຂ້ອຍຮູ້ສຶກດີຂຶ້ນ/ ເຈັບກ່ວາເກົ່າ

I've been vaccinated.
khàwy dâi sák yáa pâwng kạn lâew
ຂ້ອຍໄດ້ສັກຢາປ້ອງ ກັນແລ້ວ

I have high/low blood pressure.
khàwy míi khwáam dạn lêuat sŭung/tam
ຂ້ອຍມີຄວາມດັນ ເລືອດສູງ/ຕ່ຳ

I have my own syringe.
khàwy míi sá-léng sak yáa suan tua
ຂ້ອຍມີສະແລ້ງສັກຢາ ສ່ວນຕົວ

I'm ...	khàwy pẹn ...	ຂ້ອຍເປັນ ...
diabetic	lôhk bạo wăan	ໂລກເບົາຫວານ
asthmatic	lôhk héut	ໂລກຫືດ
anaemic	lôhk lêuat jạang	ໂລກເລືອດຈາງ

I'm allergic to ...	khàwy phâe ...	ຂ້ອຍແພ້ ...
antibiotics	yáa tâan sêua	ຢາຕ້ານເຊື້ອ
aspirin	áet-sá-pẹh-lín	ແອສເປລິນ
penicillin	pẹh-níi-síi-lín	ເປນີຊີລິນ

AT THE DENTIST

ຢູ່ທັນຕະແພດ

I have a toothache.
khàwy jép khàew — ຂ້ອຍເຈັບແຂ້ວ

I have a cavity.
khàwy pẹn khàew máeng — ຂ້ອຍເປັນແຂ້ວແມງ

I need a filling.
khàwy tâwng-kạan át khàew — ຂ້ອຍຕ້ອງການອັດແຂ້ວ

I've broken my tooth.
khàew khàwy tàek — ແຂ້ວຂ້ອຍແຕກ

My gums hurt.
khàwy jép hèuak — ຂ້ອຍເຈັບເຫືອກ

I don't want it extracted.
khàwy baw yàak lok khàew — ຂ້ອຍບໍ່ຢາກລົກແຂ້ວ

Please give me an anaesthetic.
suay sai yáa méun hài dae — ຊ່ວຍໃສ່ຢາມຶນໃຫ້ແດ່

Ouch! ọhy ໂອຍ

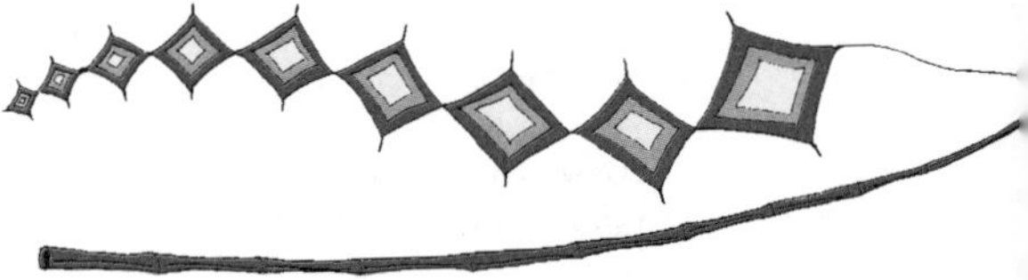

ຄວາມຕ້ອງການສະເພາະ SPECIFIC NEEDS

DISABLED TRAVELLERS ນັກທ່ອງທ່ຽວພິການ

I'm disabled.
khàwy pẹn khón phi-kạan — ຂ້ອຍເປັນຄົນພິການ

I need assistance.
khàwy tâwng-kạan khwáam suay lĕua — ຂ້ອຍຕ້ອງການຄວາມຊ່ວຍເຫລືອ

What services do you have for disabled people?
jâo bạw-li-kạan nyăng dae săm-láp khón phi-kạan — ເຈົ້າບໍລິການຫຍັງແດ່ສຳລັບຄົນພິການ

Is there wheelchair access?
kạo-îi lâw kháo pại dâi baw — ເກົ້າອີ້ລໍ້ເຂົ້າໄປໄດ້ບໍ່

Can you bring me a wheelchair?
jâo ạo kạo-îi lâw máa hap khàwy dâi baw — ເຈົ້າເອົາເກົ້າອີ້ລໍ້ມາຮັບຂ້ອຍໄດ້ບໍ່

I'm deaf.
khàwy hŭu nùak — ຂ້ອຍຫູໜວກ

I have a hearing aid.
khàwy míi kheuang suay fáng — ຂ້ອຍມີເຄື່ອງຊ່ວຍຟັງ

Speak more loudly, please.
ká-lu-náa wâo dạng-dạng dae — ກະລຸນາເວົ້າດັງໆແດ່

Are guide dogs permitted?
măa suay khon tạa bàwt á-nu-nyâat baw — ໝາຊ່ວຍຄົນຕາບອດອະນຸຍາດບໍ່

disabled person	khón phi-kạan	ຄົນພິການ
guide dog	măa suay khón tạa bàwt	ໝາຊ່ວຍຄົນຕາບອດ
wheelchair	kạo îi lâw	ເກົ້າອີ້ລໍ້

TRAVELLING WITH THE FAMILY

ເດີນທາງກັບຄອບຄົວ

Are there facilities for babies?
  míi sing ạm-núay khwáam
  sá-dùak sǎm-láp dék baw
  ມີສິ່ງອຳນວຍຄວາມ
  ສະດວກສຳລັບເດັກບໍ່

Do you have a child-minding service?
  míi bạw-li-kạan dụu láe
  dék nâwy baw
  ມີບໍລິການດູ
  ແລເດັກນ້ອຍບໍ່

Where can I find a ... -speaking babysitter? [insert country name from page 50]
  khàwy já hǎa khón lîang
  dék thii hûu pháa-sǎa
  ... dâi yuu sǎi
  ຂ້ອຍຈະຫາຄົນລ້ຽງ
  ເດັກທີ່ຮູ້ພາສາ
  ... ໄດ້ຢູ່ໃສ

Can you put an extra bed/cot in the room?
  suay sǒem tịang nái hàwng
  hài dae dâi baw
  ຊ່ວຍເສີມຕຽງ
  ໃນຫ້ອງໃຫ້ແດ່ໄດ້ບໍ່

I need a car with a child seat.
  khàwy tâwng-kạan lot thii míi
  bawn nâng sǎm-láp dék nâwy
  ຂ້ອຍຕ້ອງການລົດທີ່ມີ
  ບ່ອນນັ່ງສຳລັບເດັກນ້ອຍ

Is it suitable for children?
  mán máw-sǒm sǎm-láp
  dèk nâwy baw
  ມັນເໝາະສົມສຳລັບ
  ເດັກນ້ອຍບໍ່

Is there a family discount?
  míi suan lut láa-kháa
  sǎm-láp khâwp khúa baw
  ມີສ່ວນລຸດລາຄາ
  ສຳລັບຄອບຄົວບໍ່

Do you have a children's menu?
  míi láai-kạan ạa-hǎan
  dék nâwy baw
  ມີລາຍການອາຫານ
  ເດັກນ້ອຍບໍ່

Are there any activities for children?
  míi kít-já-kạm sǎm-láp
  dék nâwy baw
  ມີກິດຈະກຳສຳລັບ
  ເດັກນ້ອຍບໍ່

LOOKING FOR A JOB ການຊອກຫາງານທຳ

Where can I find local job advertisements?
  khàwy já sâwk hǎa pá-kàat hap sá-mak ngáan khó-sá-náa dâi yuu sǎi
  ຂ້ອຍຈະຊອກຫາ ປະກາດຮັບສະມັກງານ ໂຄສະນາໄດ້ຢູ່ໃສ

Do I need a work permit?
  khàwy tâwng-kąan míi bại á-nu-nyâat het wîak baw
  ຂ້ອຍຕ້ອງການມີໃບ ອະນຸຍາດເຮັດວຽກບໍ່

I've had experience.
  khàwy míi pá-sóp-kąan
  ຂ້ອຍມີປະສົບການ

I've come about the position advertised.
  khàwy máa pheua tąm-naeng thii dâi khó-sá-náa
  ຂ້ອຍມາເພື່ອຕຳແໜ່ງ ທີ່ໄດ້ໂຄສະນາ

I'm ringing about the position advertised.
  khàwy thóh máa kiaw-káp tąm-naeng thii dâi khó-sá-náa
  ຂ້ອຍໂທມາກ່ຽວກັບ ຕຳແໜ່ງທີ່ໄດ້ໂຄສະນາ

What's the wage?
  ngóen dẹuan thao dại
  ເງິນເດືອນເທົ່າໃດ

Do I have to pay tax?
  khàwy tâwng sǐa pháa-sǐi baw
  ຂ້ອຍຕ້ອງເສຍພາສີບໍ່

I can start ...	khàwy sǎa-mâat loem ...	ຂ້ອຍສາມາດ ເລີ່ມ ...
today	mêu nîi	ມື້ນີ້
tomorrow	mêu eun	ມື້ອື່ນ
next week	ąa-thit nàa	ອາທິດໜ້າ

Useful Words ຄຳສັບທີ່ເປັນປະໂຫຍດ

casual	thám-ma-dąa	ທຳມະດາ
employee	lûuk jâang	ລູກຈ້າງ
employer	náai jâang	ນາຍຈ້າງ
full-time	tęm wéh-láa	ເຕັມເວລາ
job	wîak	ວຽກ
occupation/trade	ąa-sîip	ອາຊີບ
part-time	khoeng wéh-láa	ເຄິ່ງເວລາ
resume/cv	síi-wa pá-wat yàw	ຊີວະປະຫວັດຫຍໍ້
traineeship	théun kąan féuk óp-hóm	ທຶນການຝຶກອົບຮົມ
work experience	pá-sóp-kąan het wîak	ປະສົບການເຮັດວຽກ

ON BUSINESS ດຳເນີນທຸລະກິດ

We're attending a ...	phûak háo khào huam ...	ພວກເຮົາ ເຂົ້າຮ່ວມ ...
conference	kąwng pá-súm sǎm-ma-náa	ກອງປະຊຸມ ສຳມະນາ
meeting	pá-súm	ປະຊຸມ
trade fair	ngáan wáang sá-dąeng sǐn khâa	ງານວາງ ສະແດງສິນຄ້າ
workshop/seminar	sǎm-ma-náa	ສຳມະນາ

I'm on a course.
khàwy kąm-láng hían
ຂ້ອຍກຳລັງຮຽນ

I have an appointment with ...
khàwy míi nat káp ...
ຂ້ອຍມີນັດກັບ ...

Here's my business card.
nîi maen bát thu-la-kít khǎwng khàwy
ນີ້ແມ່ນບັດທຸລະກິດ ຂອງຂ້ອຍ

I need an interpreter.
khàwy tâwng-kąan phùu pąe pháa-sǎa
ຂ້ອຍຕ້ອງການຜູ້ ແປພາສາ

I'd like to use a computer.
khàwy yàak sâi kháwm-pịi-tọe ຂ້ອຍຢາກໃຊ້ຄອມປີເຕີ
I'd like to send [a fax; an email].
khàwy yàak song fáek/ịi-máew ຂ້ອຍຢາກສົ່ງແຟກ/ອີແມວ

Useful Words ຄຳສັບທີ່ເປັນປະໂຫຍດ

mobile phone	thóh-la-sáp méu thĕu	ໂທລະສັບມືຖື
client	lûuk khâa	ລູກຄ້າ
colleague	pheuan huam ngáan	ເພື່ອນຮ່ວມງານ
distributor	phùu jạm-naai	ຜູ້ຈັດຈຳໜ່າຍ
email	ịi-máew	ອີແມວ
exhibition	ngáan wáang sá-dạeng	ງານວາງສະແດງ
manager	phùu ját kạan	ຜູ້ຈັດການ
profit	kạm-lái	ກຳໄລ
proposal	khàw sá-nŏe	ຂໍ້ສະເໜີ

ON TOUR ມາທ່ອງທ່ຽວ

We're part of a group.
phûak háo maen ká-lup ພວກເຮົາແມ່ນກະລຸບ
We're on tour.
phûak háo het thúa ພວກເຮົາເຮັດທົວ

I'm with the ...	máa káp ...	ມາກັບ ...
group	ká-lup	ກະລຸບ
band	wóng dọn-tịi	ວົງດົນຕີ
team	kha-na phùu lìn	ຄະນະຜູ້ຫລິ້ນ
crew	phûak lûuk méu	ພວກລູກມື

Please speak with our manager.
ká-lu-náa lóm káp phùu ját kạan phûak háo ກະລຸນາລົມກັບຜູ້ຈັດການພວກເຮົາ
We've lost our equipment.
phûak háo het kheuang ú-pá-kạwn sĭa ພວກເຮົາເຮັດເຄື່ອງອຸປະກອນເສຍ

SPECIFIC NEEDS

We sent equipment on this ...	phûak háo song kheuang ú-pá-kạwn tháang ...	ພວກເຮົາສົ່ງເຄື່ອງອຸປະກອນທາງ ...
flight	thìaw bịn	ຖ້ຽວບິນ
bus	lot méh	ລົດເມ

We're taking a break of ... days.
phûak háo phak kạan ... mêu ພວກເຮົາພັກການ ... ມື້

We're playing on ...
phûak háo já lìn ... ພວກເຮົາຈະຫລິ້ນ ...

FILM & TV CREWS ຄະນະຖ່າຍທຳແລະຄະນະຖ່າຍທຳໂທລະພາບ

We're on location.
phûak háo yuu thii sá-thăan thii thaai thám ພວກເຮົາຢູ່ທີ່ສະຖານທີ່ຖ່າຍທຳ

We're filming!
kạam-láng thaai thám ກຳລັງຖ່າຍທຳ

May we film here?
thaai thám yuu nîi dâi baw ຖ່າຍທຳຢູ່ນີ້ໄດ້ບໍ່

We're making a ...	phûak háo thaai ...	ພວກເຮົາຖ່າຍ ...
documentary	fím èhk-á-săan	ຟິມເອກະສານ
film	năng leuang	ໜັງເລື່ອງ
TV series	tạwn thóh-la-thát	ຕອນໂທລະທັດ

DID YOU KNOW ...

Buddhism is practised by approximately 60% of the Lao population; animism and other religions make up the remainder.

PILGRIMAGE & RELIGION ການເຄົາລົບບູຊາແລະສາສະນາ

I'm ...	khàwy thĕu ...	ຂ້ອຍຖື ...
Buddhist	sàat-sá-náa phut	ສາສະນາພຸດ
Christian	sàat-sá-náa khlit	ສາສະນາຄລິດ
Hindu	sàat-sá-náa hín-dụu	ສາສະນາຮິນດູ
Jewish	sàat-sá-náa yíu	ສາສະນາຢິວ
Muslim	sàat-sá-náa mu-sá-lím	ສາສະນາມຸສລິມ

I'm not religious.
khàwy baw thĕu sàat-sá-náa — ຂ້ອຍບໍ່ຖືສາສະນາ

I'm (Catholic), but not practising.
khàwy maen (kạa-tọh-lik) tae baw dâi thĕu — ຂ້ອຍແມ່ນ (ກາໂຕລິກ) ແຕ່ບໍ່ໄດ້ນັບຖື

I think I believe in God.
khit waa seua thĕu pha-phùu pẹn jâo — ຄິດວ່າເຊື່ອຖືພະຜູ້ເປັນເຈົ້າ

I believe in destiny.
khàwy seua thĕu sá-tạa-kạm — ຂ້ອຍເຊື່ອຖືສະຕາກັມ

I'm interested in astrology/philosophy.
khàwy sŏn jại hŏ-la-sàat/pát-sá-yáa — ຂ້ອຍສົນໃຈໂຫລະສາດ/ປັດສະຍາ

I'm an atheist.
khàwy baw seua thĕu pha-phùu pẹn jâo — ຂ້ອຍບໍ່ເຊື່ອຖືພະຜູ້ເປັນເຈົ້າ

I'm agnostic.
khàwy seua thĕu thám-ma-dàa — ຂ້ອຍເຊື່ອຖືທຳມະດາ

Can I attend this ceremony?
khàwy săa-mâat khào huam phi-thíi nîi dâi baw — ຂ້ອຍສາມາດເຂົ້າຮ່ວມພິທີນີ້ໄດ້ບໍ່

Can I pray here?
 sùut món yuu nîi dâi baw — ສູດມົນຢູ່ນີ້ໄດ້ບໍ່
Where can I pray?
 khàwy sǎa-mâat sùut món dâi yuu sǎi — ຂ້ອຍສາມາດສູດມົນໄດ້ຢູ່ໃສ

Buddhist temple; monastery	wat	ວັດ
church	bòht khlit	ໂບດຄລິດ
funeral	ngáan	ງານ
	sáa-pạa-na-kít sóp	ຊາປານະກິດຊົບ
god	pha jâo	ພະເຈົ້າ
monk	khuu-bạa, nak bùat	ຄູບາ ນັກບວດ
prayer	kạan sùut món	ການສູດມົນ
priest	khún phaw (nái sàat-sá-náa khlit)	ຄຸນພໍ່ (ໃນສາສະນາຄລິດ)
religious ceremony	phi-thíi kạm sàat-sá-náa	ພິທີກຳສາສະນາ
sabbath	wán sǐn	ວັນສິນ
saint	khón jại pha	ຄົນໃຈພະ
shrine	hǎw wài	ຫໍໄຫວ້
stupa	thâat	ທາດ

A LITTLE IN US ALL ...

The traditional religion of Laos is animism – the belief that a soul or spirit can be found in all objects, animate or inanimate. Practice of these beliefs can still be seen today at Wat Si Muang in Vientiene. Here, the central image of the temple is the city pillar, where the city's guardian spirit is said to reside.

TRACING ROOTS & HISTORY
ຊອກຄົ້ນຫາ ບັນພະບູລຸດ ແລະ ປະຫວັດສາດ

I think my ancestors came from this area.

khit waa bạn-pha-bụu-lút khǎwng khàwy máa jàak bạw-li-wéhn nîi	ຄິດວ່າບັນພະບູລຸດຂອງຂ້ອຍມາຈາກບໍລິເວນນີ້

I'm looking for my relatives.

khàwy sâwk hǎa phii-nâwng khǎwng khàwy	ຂ້ອຍຊອກຫາພີ່ນ້ອງຂອງຂ້ອຍ

I have a relative who lives around here.

khàwy míi phii-nâwng yuu thii nîi	ຂ້ອຍມີພີ່ນ້ອງຢູ່ທີ່ນີ້

Is there anyone here by the name of ...?

yuu nîi míi khón seu ...	ຢູ່ນີ້ມີຄົນຊື່ ...

I'd like to go to the burial ground.

khàwy yàak pại bawn fǎng sóp	ຂ້ອຍຢາກໄປບ່ອນຝັງຊົບ

My (father) was stationed here during the Indochina War.

nái pạang sǒng-kháam ịn-dụu-jịin phaw khǎwng khàwy dâi pá-jạm yuu thii nîi	ໃນປາງສົງຄາມອິນດູຈີນພໍ່ຂອງຂ້ອຍໄດ້ປະຈຳຢູ່ທີ່ນີ້

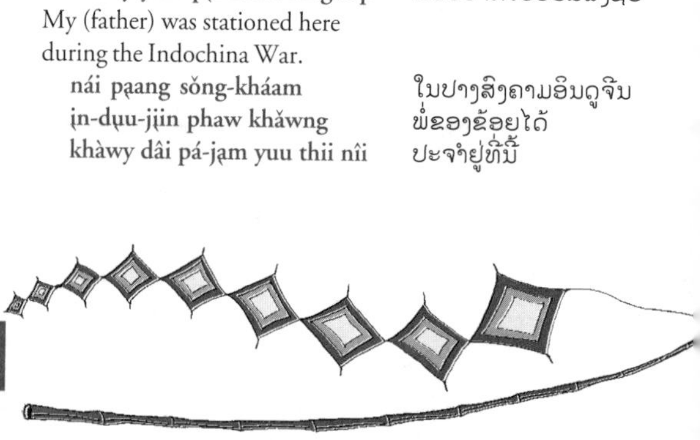

ເວລາ, ວັນທີ ແລະ ເທດສະການ — TIME, DATES & FESTIVALS

TIME ເວລາ

The Lao tell time using a 12-hour system that divides the day into four sections (ຕອນ, tąwn). The 'dead of night' period (11 pm to 6 am) is known as kąang khéun (ກາງຄືນ).

6 am to noon	tąwn sâo	ຕອນເຊົ້າ
noon to 3 or 4 pm	tąwn baai	ຕອນບ່າຍ
3 or 4 pm to 6 pm	tąwn láeng	ຕອນແລງ
6 to 11 pm	tąwn khám	ຕອນຄ່ຳ

Clock time is expressed in móhng (ໂມງ, hour) and náa-thíi (ນາທີ, minutes), plus one of the above times of day. When speaking, baai (ບ່າຍ, afternoon) comes before the hour; all the other times of day come after.

What time is it?	wéh-láa ják móhng	ເວລາຈັກໂມງ

9 am	kâo móhng sâo	ເກົ້າໂມງເຊົ້າ
midday	thiang	ທ່ຽງ
1 pm	baai móhng	ບ່າຍໂມງ
2.15 pm	baai săwng móhng síp-hàa	ບ່າຍສອງໂມງ ສິບຫ້າ
5 pm	hàa móhng láeng	ຫ້າໂມງແລງ
8.20 pm	pàet móhng sáo tąwn khám	ແປດໂມງຊາວ ຕອນຄ່ຳ
midnight	thiang khéun	ທ່ຽງຄືນ

When expressing time in terms of number of hours, use sua-móhng (ຊົ່ວໂມງ) rather than móhng.

three hours	săam sua-móhng	ສາມຊົ່ວໂມງ

DAYS OF THE WEEK ວັນໃນສັບປະດາ

Sunday	wán ąa-thit	ວັນອາທິດ
Monday	wán jąn	ວັນຈັນ
Tuesday	wán ąng-kháan	ວັນອັງຄານ
Wednesday	wán phut	ວັນພຸດ
Thursday	wán pha-hát	ວັນພະຫັດ
Friday	wán súk	ວັນສຸກ
Saturday	wán săo	ວັນເສົາ

week	ąa-thit	ອາທິດ
weekend	săo-ąa-thit	ເສົາອາທິດ

MONTHS ເດືອນ

January	dęuan máng-kąwn	ເດືອນມັງກອນ
February	dęuan kųm-pháa	ເດືອນກຸມພາ
March	dęuan mi-náa	ເດືອນມີນາ
April	dęuan méh-săa	ເດືອນເມສາ
May	dęuan pheut-sá-pháa	ເດືອນພຶດສະພາ
June	dęuan mi-thú-náa	ເດືອນມິຖຸນາ
July	dęuan kąw-la-kót	ເດືອນກໍລະກົດ
August	dęuan sĭng-hăa	ເດືອນສິງຫາ
September	dęuan kąn-yáa	ເດືອນກັນຍາ
October	dęuan tú-láa	ເດືອນຕຸລາ
November	dęuan pha-jík	ເດືອນພະຈິກ
December	dęuan than-wáa	ເດືອນທັນວາ

month	dęuan	ເດືອນ
half a month	khoeng dęuan	ເຄິ່ງເດືອນ
a month and a half	dęuan khoeng	ເດືອນເຄິ່ງ

SEASONS ລະດູ

hot season; dry season (Mar-May)
  la-dụu hâwn; la-dụu lâeng — ລະດູຮ້ອນ/ລະດູແລ້ງ
rainy season (Jun-Oct)
  la-dụu fŏn — ລະດູຝົນ
cool season (Nov-Feb)
  la-dụu năo — ລະດູໜາວ

DATES ວັນທີ

The traditional Lao calendar, like the calendars of China, Vietnam, Cambodia and Thailand, is a solar-lunar mix. The year itself is reckoned by solar phases, while the months are divided according to lunar phases (unlike the Gregorian calendar in which months as well as years are reckoned by the sun). The Lao Buddhist Era (BE) calendar figures year one as 543 BC, which means that you must subtract 543 from the Lao calendar year to arrive at the 'Christian era' (Gregorian) calendar familiar in the West (eg, AD 2001 is 2544 BE according to the Lao Buddhist calendar).

Most educated Lao are also familiar with the 'Christian era' (khit sák-á-lâat) calendar.

2544 (BE)
  (pháw săw) săwng phán hàa hâwy sii-síp sii — ສອງພັນຫ້າຮ້ອຍສີ່ສິບສີ່
2001 (AD)
  (kháw săw) săwng phán neung — ສອງພັນໜຶ່ງ

Days of the month are numbered according to the familiar Gregorian calendar.

13th January
  wán thíi síp-săam dẹuan máng-kạwn — ວັນທີສິບສາມເດືອນມັງກອນ

date	wán thíi	ວັນທີ
year	pịi	ປີ
What date?	wán thíi thao-dại?	ວັນທີເທົ່າໃດ

PRESENT ປະຈຸບັນ

today	mêu nîi	ມື້ນີ້
this evening	láeng nîi	ແລງນີ້
tonight	khéun nîi	ຄືນນີ້
this morning	sâo nîi	ເຊົ້ານີ້
this afternoon	baai nîi	ບ່າຍນີ້
this month	dẹuan nîi	ເດືອນນີ້
all day long	ta-làwt mêu	ຕະຫລອດມື້

PAST ອາດີດ

yesterday	mêu wáan nîi	ມື້ວານນີ້
the day before yesterday	mêu séun	ມື້ຊືນ
last week	ạa-thit lâew	ອາທິດແລ້ວ
two weeks ago	sǎwng ạa-thit lâew	ສອງອາທິດແລ້ວ
three months ago	sǎam dẹuan lâew	ສາມເດືອນແລ້ວ
four years ago	kawn nîi sii pị	ກ່ອນນີ້ສີ່ປີ

FUTURE ອະນາຄົດ

tomorrow	mêu eun	ມື້ອື່ນ
the day after tomorrow	mêu héu	ມື້ຮື
next week	ạa-thit nàa	ອາທິດໜ້າ
next month	dẹuan nàa	ເດືອນໜ້າ
two more months	ìik sǎwng dẹuan	ອີກສອງເດືອນ

TENSE TONES

You don't need to worry about speaking in the right tense to speak Lao grammatically, but if you want to be understood, remember that Lao is a tonal language – so always be aware that you have to avoid English intonation, such as raising your voice at the end of a question (see page 17 for more help with this).

FESTIVALS & NATIONAL HOLIDAYS ເທດສະການ ທາງການແລະວັນພັກ

Festivals in Laos are mostly linked to agricultural seasons or historical Buddhist holidays. The general word for festival in Lao is **bụn** (ບຸນ, often written as *boun)*. Exact dates for festivals may vary from year to year, either because of the lunar calendar – which isn't quite in sync with the Gregorian solar calendar – or because local authorities decide to change festival dates.

On dates noted as public holidays, all government offices and banks will be closed.

February

Magha Puja ma-khà bụu-sáa ມະຄະບູຊາ

This day is celebrated on the full moon of the third lunar month to commemorate the preaching of the Buddha to 1250 enlightened monks who came to hear him 'without prior summons'. A public holiday throughout the country, it culminates in a candle-lit walk around the main chapel at every wat.

Late January to early March

Chinese New Year; Vietnamese Tet kút jịin ກຸດຈີນ

Chinese and Vietnamese populations all over Laos celebrate their lunar new year (the date shifts from year to year) with a week of house-cleaning, lion dances and fireworks. The most impressive festivities take place in Vientiane, Pakse and Savannakhet, with parties, deafening nonstop fireworks and visits to Vietnamese and Chinese temples. Chinese- and Vietnamese-run businesses usually close for three days.

April

Lao New Year pị̀i mai láo ປີໃໝ່ລາວ

The lunar new year begins in mid-April and practically the entire country comes to a halt and celebrates. Houses are cleaned, people put on new clothes and Buddha images are washed with lustral water. In the wats, offerings of fruit and flowers are made at various altars and votive mounds of sand or stone are fashioned in the courtyards. Later the citizens take to the streets and dowse one another with water, which is an appropriate activity as April is usually the hottest month of the year. This festival is particularly picturesque in Luang Prabang, where it includes elephant processions. The 15th, 16th and 17th of April are official public holidays.

May (Full Moon)

Visakha Puja wi-săa-khá bụu-sáa ວິສາຂະບູຊາ

This public holiday falls on the 15th day of the waxing moon in the sixth lunar month. It is considered the date of the Buddha's birth, enlightenment and parinibbana, or passing away. Activities are centred around the wat, with candle-lit processions, much chanting and sermonising.

Rocket Festival bụn bâng fái ບຸນບັ້ງໄຟ

This is a pre-Buddhist rain ceremony that is now celebrated alongside Visakha Puja in Laos and north-east Thailand. This can be one of the wildest festivals in the country, with plenty of music and dance (especially the irreverent măw lám (ໝໍລຳ) performances) processions and general merrymaking, culminating in the firing of bamboo rockets into the sky. In some places, male participants blacken their bodies with lamp soot, while women wear sunglasses and carry carved wooden phalli to imitate men. The firing of the rockets is supposed to prompt the heavens to initiate the rainy season and bring much-needed water to the rice fields.

July

Asanha Puja ąa-săn-há bųu-sáa ອາສັນຫະບູຊາ

This public holiday commemorates the first sermon preached by the Buddha.

Mid to late July (Full Moon)

Rains Retreat Opening khào phán-săa (khào wat-săa) ເຂົ້າພັນສາ (ເຂົ້າວັດສາ)

This is the beginning of the traditional three-month 'rains retreat', during which Buddhist monks are expected to station themselves in a single monastery. At other times of year they are allowed to travel from wat to wat or simply to wander in the countryside, but during the rainy season they forego the wandering so as not to damage fields of rice or other crops. This is also the traditional time of year for men to enter the monkhood temporarily, hence many ordinations take place.

August/September (Full Moon)

Ancestor Respect haw khào pá-dáp dįn ຫໍ່ເຂົ້າປະດັບດິນ

This is a sombre festival in which the living pay respect to the dead. Many cremations take place during this time and gifts are presented to the Sangha (Buddhist clergy) so that monks will chant on behalf of the deceased. Families visit bone stupas (ທາດກະດູກ, thàat ká-dùuk) with offerings of candles, incense and flowers.

October/November (Full Moon)

Rains Retreat Closing — àwk phán-săa (àwk wat-săa) — ອອກພັນສາ (ອອກວັດສາ)

This celebrates the end of the 3-month Rains Retreat. Monks are allowed to leave the monasteries to travel and are presented with robes, alms-bowls and other requisites of the renunciative life. A second festival held in association with Awk Phansaa is the **Bụn Nâam** (Water Festival). Boat races are commonly held in towns located on rivers, such as Vientiane, Luang Prabang and Savannakhet.

Pha That Luang Festival — bụn pha thâat lŭang — ບຸນພະທາດຫລວງ

This takes place at Pha That Luang in Vientiane. Hundreds of monks assemble to receive alms and floral votives early in the morning on the first day of the festival, and there's a colourful procession between Pha That Luang and Wat Si Muang. The celebration lasts a week and includes fireworks and music, culminating in a candlelit circumambulation of That Luang.

December

Lao National Day — wán sâat láo — ວັນຊາດລາວ

The 2nd of December marks the 1975 victory of the proletariat over the monarchy with parades and speeches. It is a public holiday.

December/January

Prince Vessantara Festival **bụn pha wêht** ບຸນພະເວດ

This is a temple-centred festival in which the *jataka* or birth-tale of Prince Vessantara, the Buddha's penultimate life, is recited. This is also a favoured time (second to **khào phán-săa**) for Lao males to be ordained into the monkhood. The scheduling of Bun Pha Wet is staggered so that it is held on different days in different villages. This is so that relatives and friends living in different villages can invite one another to their respective celebrations.

New Year's Day **wán pịi mai săa-kọn** ວັນປີໃໝ່ສາກົນ

A recent public holiday in deference to the Western calendar.

Useful Words & Phrases

ບາງຄຳສັບແລະປະໂຫຍກທີ່ເປັນປະໂຫຍດ

always	lêuay lêuay	ເລື້ອຍໆ
annual	thuk pịi	ທຸກປີ
before	kawn	ກອນ
century	sá-tá-wat	ສະຕະວັດ
closed	pít	ປິດ
dawn	tạa-wán khèun	ຕາວັນຂຶ້ນ
daytime	kạang wán	ກາງວັນ
early	sâo	ເຊົ້າ
evening	láeng	ແລງ
every day	thuk wán	ທຸກວັນ
forever	tá-làwt kạan	ຕະຫລອດການ
holiday	wán phak kạan	ວັນພັກການ
late	sâa	ຊ້າ
night	khám	ຄ່ຳ
now	diaw nîi; tạwn nîi	ດຽວນີ້/ຕອນນີ້
nowadays	sá-măi nîi	ສະໄໝນີ້
open	pòet	ເປີດ
period (era)	sá-măi	ສະໄໝ
period (interval)	wéh-láa	ເວລາ
sometimes	bạang theua	ບາງເທື່ອ
time	wéh-láa	ເວລາ
on time	kọng taw wéh-láa	ກົງຕໍ່ເວລາ
in time	seu wéh-láa	ຊື່ເວລາ
until	jọn kwaa	ຈົນກ່ວາ
when (conjunction)	mêua/wéh-láa	ເມື່ອ/ເວລາ
when (what date?)	mêua-dại	ເມື່ອໃດ
whenever	mêua-dại kaw-tạam	ເມື່ອໃດກໍ່ຕາມ

NUMBERS & AMOUNTS

ນຳເບີ້ແລະຈຳນວນ

See the Grammar section for important information on how to use 'classifiers' or 'counters' with Lao numbers.

CARDINAL NUMBERS ເລກນັບ

zero	sǔun	ສູນ
one	neung	ໜຶ່ງ
two	sǎwng	ສອງ
three	sǎam	ສາມ
four	sii	ສີ່
five	hàa	ຫ້າ
six	hók	ຫົກ
seven	jét	ເຈັດ
eight	pàet	ແປດ
nine	kâo	ເກົ້າ
10	síp	ສິບ
11	síp-ét	ສິບເອັດ
12	síp-sǎwng	ສິບສອງ
13	síp-sǎam	ສິບສາມ
14	síp-sii	ສິບສີ່
...-teen	síp-...	ສິບ ...
20	sáo	ຊາວ
21	sáo-ét	ຊາວເອັດ
22	sáo-sǎwng	ຊາວສອງ
23	sáo-sǎam	ຊາວສາມ
30	sǎam-síp	ສາມສິບ
40	sii-síp	ສີ່ສິບ
50	hàa-síp	ຫ້າສິບ
60	hók-síp	ຫົກສິບ
70	jét-síp	ເຈັດສິບ
80	pàet-síp	ແປດສິບ
90	kâo-síp	ເກົ້າສິບ

100	hâwy	ຮ້ອຍ
200	săwng hâwy	ສອງຮ້ອຍ
300	săam hâwy	ສາມຮ້ອຍ
1000	phán	ພັນ
10,000	meun (síp-phán)	ໝື່ນ (ສິບພັນ)
100,000	săen (hâwy phán)	ແສນ (ຮ້ອຍພັນ)
million	lâan	ລ້ານ
billion	têu (phan láan)	ຕື້

ORDINAL NUMBERS ເລກລຳດັບ

These are formed by adding thíi (ທີ່) before the cardinal numbers.

first	thíi neung	ທີ່ໜຶ່ງ
second	thíi sǎwng	ທີ່ສອງ
thirty-first	thíi sǎam-síp-ét	ທີ່ສາມສິບເອັດ

FRACTIONS ເລກສ່ວນ

Fractions are formed by inserting suan (ສ່ວນ, part) before the lower integer. 'Half' has its own term, khoeng (ເຄິ່ງ).

one quarter (1/4)	neung suan sii	ໜຶ່ງສ່ວນສີ່
one eighth (1/8)	neung suan pàet	ໜຶ່ງສ່ວນແປດ
three eighths (3/8)	sǎam suan pàet	ສາມສ່ວນແປດ
half (1/2)	khoeng	ເຄິ່ງ

Useful Words ບາງຄຳສັບທີ່ເປັນປະໂຫຍດ

count	nap	ນັບ
couple/pair	khuu	ຄູ່
decimal point	jút	ຈຸດ
dozen	lǒh	ໂຫລ
equal (adj)	thao kạn	ເທົ່າກັນ
equal to	thao káp	ເທົ່າກັບ
large	nyai	ໃຫຍ່
least	nâwy thii-sút	ນ້ອຍທີ່ສຸດ
little/few	nâwy	ນ້ອຍ
many	lǎai	ຫລາຍ

minus	lop	ລົບ
most	lǎai thii-sút	ຫລາຍທີ່ສຸດ
much	lǎai	ຫລາຍ
number (amount)	jąm-núan	ຈຳນວນ
number (numeral)	nâm-bọe (lêhk)	ນ້ຳເບີ້(ເລກ)
plus	pá-sǒm/buak	ປະສົມ/ບວກ
small	nâwy	ນ້ອຍ
weight	nâm-nak	ນ້ຳໜັກ

ສຸກເສີນ EMERGENCIES

Help!	suay dae	ຊ່ວຍແດ່
It's an emergency!	súk sŏen	ສຸກເສີນ
Stop!	yút	ຢຸດ
Go away!	nĭi pại	ໜີໄປ
Watch out!	la-wáng	ລະວັງ
Thief!	khá-móhy (jọhn)	ຂະໂມຍ (ໂຈນ)
Fire!	fái mài	ໄຟໄໝ້

There's been an accident!
    míi ú-bát-tí-het   ມີອຸບັດຕິເຫດ

Call a doctor!
    suay ôen thaan măw hài dae   ຊ່ວຍເອີ້ນທ່ານໝໍໃຫ້ແດ່

Call an ambulance!
    suay ôen lot hóhng măw dae   ຊ່ວຍເອີ້ນລົດໂຮງໝໍແດ່

Call the police!
    suay ôen tam-lùat dae   ຊ່ວຍເອີ້ນຕຳຫລວດແດ່

I've been robbed.
    khàwy thèuk khá-móhy   ຂ້ອຍຖືກຂະໂມຍ

I've been raped.
    khàwy thèuk khòm khĕun   ຂ້ອຍຖືກຂົ່ມຂືນ

I'll get the police.
    khàwy sii oên tam-lùat   ຂ້ອຍຊິເອີ້ນຕຳຫລວດ

Useful Phrases ປະໂຫຍກທີ່ເປັນປະໂຫຍດ

Could you help me please?
jâo suay khàwy dâi baw ເຈົ້າຊ່ວຍຂ້ອຍໄດ້ບໍ່
I am ill.
khàwy puay ຂ້ອຍປ່ວຍ
I have health insurance.
khàwy míi pá-kạn phái sú-khá-phâap ຂ້ອຍມີປະກັນໄພສຸຂະພາບ
My blood group is (A, B, O, AB) positive/negative.
lêuat khàwy maen klúp (A, B, O, AB) bùak/lop ເລືອດຂ້ອຍແມ່ນກລຸບ (A, B, O, AB) ບວກ/ລົບ
I am lost.
khàwy lŏng tháang ຂ້ອຍຫລົງທາງ
Where are the toilets?
hàwng nâm yuu săi ຫ້ອງນ້ຳຢູ່ໃສ
Could I please use the telephone?
sâi thóh-la-sáp dâi baw ໃຊ້ໂທລະສັບໄດ້ບໍ່

POLICE ຕຳຫລວດ

Where's the police station?
sa-thăa-níi tam-lùat yuu săi ສະຖານີຕຳຫລວດຢູ່ໃສ

My ... was/were stolen.	... khăwng khàwy thèuk khá-móhy	... ຂອງຂ້ອຍຖືກຂະໂມຍ
I've lost my ...	khàwy het ... sĭa lâew	ຂ້ອຍເຮັດ ... ເສຍແລ້ວ
bags	kọng kheuang	ຖົງເຄື່ອງ
money	ngóen	ເງິນ
travellers cheques	saek dọen tháang	ແຊັກເດີນທາງ
passport	năng-sĕu phaan dạen	ໜັງສືຜ່ານແດນ

I would like to contact my embassy/consulate.
    yàak tít taw sa-thǎan-thûut khǎwng khàwy — ຢາກຕິດຕໍ່ສະຖານທູດ ຂອງຂ້ອຍ

I speak (English).
    khàwy wâo pháa-sǎa (ạng-kít) — ຂ້ອຍເວົ້າພາສາ (ອັງກິດ)

I understand.
    khàwy khào jại — ຂ້ອຍເຂົ້າໃຈ

I don't understand.
    khàwy baw khào jại — ຂ້ອຍບໍ່ເຂົ້າໃຈ

I didn't realise I was doing anything wrong.
    khàwy baw hûu dâi het nyǎng phít — ຂ້ອຍບໍ່ຮູ້ໄດ້ເຮັດ ຫຍັງຜິດ

I didn't do it.
    khàwy baw dâi het — ຂ້ອຍບໍ່ໄດ້ເຮັດ

I'm sorry, I apologise.
    khǎw thôht, sǐa jại — ຂໍໂທດເສຍໃຈ

My contact number in case of emergency (next of kin) is ...
    khâwp khúa thii já hài tít taw nái káw-la-níi súk sǒen ... — ຄອບຄົວທີ່ຈະໃຫ້ຕິດຕໍ່ໃນ ກໍລະນີສຸກເສີນ ...

A

to be able (can)	dâi	ໄດ້

> I can.
> khàwy dâi — ຂ້ອຍໄດ້
>
> I can't.
> khàwy baw dâi — ຂ້ອຍບໍ່ໄດ້
>
> Can you ...?
> jâo dâi baw ... — ເຈົ້າໄດ້ບໍ່ ...

about (approximately)	pá-máan	ປະມານ
above (adv)	tháang thóeng	ທາງເທິງ
above (prep)	yuu thóeng	ຢູ່ເທິງ
abroad	taang pá-thêht	ຕ່າງປະເທດ
to accept	hap	ຮັບ

> I accept.
> khàwy hap — ຂ້ອຍຮັບ
>
> Do you accept?
> jâo hap baw — ເຈົ້າຮັບບໍ່

accident	ú-bát-tí-hèht	ອຸບັດຕິເຫດ
accommodation	bawn phak	ບ່ອນພັກ
addiction	sèhp tít	ເສບຕິດ
address	thii yuu	ທີ່ຢູ່
administration	kạan ját tâng	ການຈັດຕັ້ງ
admission (entry)	phaan khào	ຜ່ານເຂົ້າ
admission fee	khaa phaan pá-tụu	ຄ່າຜ່ານປະຕູ
to admit (allow entry)	á-nu-nyâat khào	ອະນຸຍາດເຂົ້າ
adult	phùu nyai	ຜູ້ໃຫຍ່
adventure	pá-jọn phái	ປະຈົນໄພ
aeroplane	héua bịn	ເຮືອບິນ
by aeroplane	dọhy héua bịn	ໂດຍເຮືອບິນ
after	lăng jàak	ຫຼັງຈາກ

again	ìik	ອີກ
against	tâan	ຕ້ານ
to agree	hĕn dịi	ເຫັນດີ

I agree.		
khàwy hĕn dịi		ຂ້ອຍເຫັນດີ
Do you agree?		
jâo hĕn dịi baw		ເຈົ້າເຫັນດີບໍ່
Agreed!		
tók-lóng		ຕົກລົງ

agriculture	ká-sí-kạm	ກະສິກຳ
ahead	kawn	ກ່ອນ
aid	suay lĕua	ຊ່ວຍເຫຼືອ
AIDS	lôhk èht	ໂລກເອດສ
airline	săai kạan bịn	ສາຍການບິນ
airmail	tháang ạa-kàat	ທາງອາກາດ
by airmail	dọhy tháang ạa-kàat	ໂດຍທາງອາກາດ
alarm clock	móhng púk	ໂມງປຸກ
all	tháng mót	ທັງໝົດ
allergy	phúum phâe	ພູມແພ້
to allow	á-nu-mat	ອະນຸມັດ
almost	kèuap	ເກືອບ
alone	dòht diaw	ໂດດດ່ຽວ
also	khéu/teum	ຄື/ຕື່ມ
alternative	tháang lêuak	ທາງເລືອກ
always	lêuay lêuay	ເລື້ອຍໆ
amazing	ma-hat-sá-jạn	ມະຫັດສະຈັນ
ambassador	èhk-ák-kha-lat-thá-thûut	ເອກອັກຄະລັດຖະທູດ
ambulance	lot hóng măw	ລົດໂຮງໝໍ
among	la-waang	ລະຫວ່າງ
ancient	bọh-háan	ໂບຮານ
and	lae	ແລະ

angry	hâai	ຮ້າຍ
antique (adj)	kheuang bọh-háan	ເຄື່ອງໂບຮານ
any	eun-dại	ອື່ນໃດ
anytime	wéh-láa dại kaw dâi	ເວລາໃດກໍ່ໄດ້
apartment	ạa-kháan	ອາຄານ
appointment	kạan nat phop	ການນັດພົບ
approximately	pá-máan	ປະມານ
archaeological	bụu-háan-na-kha-dịi	ບູຮານນະຄະດີ
to argue	thók thǐang	ຖົກຖຽງ
argument	kạan thók thǐang	ການຖົກຖຽງ
to arrive	máa hâwt	ມາຮອດ
art	sǐi-la-pá	ສີລະປະ
to ask	thǎam	ຖາມ
at (place)	yuu thii	ຢູ່ທີ່
at (time)	nái wéh-láa	ໃນເວລາ
automatic	ọh-tọh-nóh-mat	ໂອໂຕໂນມັດ

B

baby	dék nâwy	ເດັກນ້ອຍ
back	lǎng	ຫລັງ
backpack	bạa-lóh; thǒng pêh	ບາໂລ; ຖົງເປ້
bad	sua	ຊົ່ວ
bag	kheuang/thǒng	ເຄື່ອງ/ຖົງ
baggage	ká-pạo kheuang	ກະເປົາເຄື່ອງ
ball (object)	màak bạan	ໝາກບານ
bank	tha-náa-kháan	ທະນາຄານ
bar	bạa	ບາ
to bathe	àap nâm	ອາບນ້ຳ
bathers (swimsuit)	sut láwy nâm	ຊຸດລອຍນ້ຳ
women's	khǎwng mae nyíng	ຂອງແມ່ຍິງ
men's	khǎwng phùu sáai	ຂອງຜູ້ຊາຍ
bathroom	hàwng nâm	ຫ້ອງນ້ຳ

B

battery	thaan fái săai; mâw fái	ຖ່ານໄຟສາຍ; ໝໍ້ໄຟ
beautiful	ngáam	ງາມ
because	phaw-waa	ເພາະວ່າ
bed	tịang	ຕຽງ
before (conj)	kawn	ກ່ອນ
before (prep)	kawn	ກ່ອນ
beggar	khón khăw tháan	ຄົນຂໍທານ
to begin	loem	ເລີ່ມ
beginner	phùu loem tôn	ຜູ້ເລີ່ມຕົ້ນ
behind	tháang lăng	ທາງຫລັງ
below (adv)	yuu lum	ຢູ່ລຸ່ມ
below (prep)	bêuang lum	ເບື້ອງລຸ່ມ
beside	khàang káp	ຂ້າງກັບ
best	dịi thii-sút	ດີທີ່ສຸດ
better	dịi kwaa	ດີກ່ວາ
between (prep)	la-waang	ລະຫວ່າງ
Bible	tạm-láa săa-sa-náa khlit	ຕຳລາສາສະນາຄລິດ
bicycle	lot thìip	ລົດຖີບ
big	nyai	ໃຫຍ່
bill	bại bịin	ໃບບິນ
birthday	wán kòet	ວັນເກີດ
to bite	kát	ກັດ
bitter	khŏm	ຂົມ
blanket	phàa hom	ຜ້າຫົ່ມ
to bless	ụay pháwn	ອວຍພອນ
blind	tạa bàwt	ຕາບອດ
blood	lêuat	ເລືອດ
boat	héua	ເຮືອ
bomb	la-bòet	ລະເບີດ

Bon appetit!
sóen sâep ເຊີນແຊບ

book	pêum	ປື້ມ
bookshop	hâan khăai pêum	ຮ້ານຂາຍປື້ມ

DICTIONARY

bored	beua naai	เบื่อหน่าย
I'm bored.		
khàwy beua		ຂ້ອຍເບື່ອ
border	sáai daen	ຊາຍແດນ
to borrow	yéum	ຢືມ
May I borrow this?		
khăw yéum dae		ຂໍຢືມແດ່
boss	náai	ນາຍ
both	tháng săwng	ທັງສອງ
bottle opener	kheuang khăi kâew	ເຄື່ອງໄຂແກ້ວ
boy	dék sáai	ເດັກຊາຍ
brake(s)	hàam	ຫ້າມ
bread	khào jii	ເຂົ້າຈີ່
to break	tàek	ແຕກ
breakfast	qa-hăan sâo	ອາຫານເຊົ້າ
to breathe	hăai jai	ຫາຍໃຈ
bribe	sĭn bon	ສິນບົນ
to bribe	hài sĭn bon	ໃຫ້ສິນບົນ
bridge	khŭa	ຂົວ
bright	jâeng	ແຈ້ງ
to bring	qo máa	ເອົາມາ
Can you bring it?		
jâo qo máa dâi baw		ເຈົ້າເອົາມາໄດ້ບໍ່
broken	phéh lâew	ເພແລ້ວ
bucket	khú sai nâm	ຂຸໃສ່ນ້ຳ
building	qa-kháan	ອາຄານ
to burn	jút/mâi	ຈຸດ/ໄໝ້
bus	lot méh	ລົດເມ
business	thu-la-kít	ທຸລະກິດ
busy	kháa wîak; nyùng	ຄາວຽກ; ຫຍຸ້ງ
but	tae waa	ແຕ່ວ່າ

to buy	sêu	ຊື້

Where did you buy this?
jâo sêu nîi máa tae săi — ເຈົ້າຊື້ ນີ້ມາແຕ່ໃສ

C

cafe	hâan kạa-féh	ຮ້ານກາເຟ
camera	kâwng thaai hûup	ກ້ອງຖ່າຍຮູບ
to camp	tâng khêm	ຕັ້ງເຄັ້ມ
can (tin)	ká-pạwng	ກະປອງ
can	dâi	ໄດ້

Can I take a photograph?
thaai hûup dâi baw — ຖ່າຍຮູບໄດ້ບໍ່

No, you can't.
baw dâi — ບໍ່ໄດ້

cancel	yok lôek	ຍົກເລີກ
can opener	kheuang khăi ká-pạwng	ເຄື່ອງໄຂກະປອງ
candle	thían	ທຽນ
capital (city)	na-kháwn lŭang	ນະຄອນຫລວງ
capitalism	théun-ni-nyom	ທຶນນິຍົມ
car	lot	ລົດ
cards (playing)	phâi	ໄພ້
to care	dụu-láe	ດູແລ

I don't care.
khàwy baw sŏn — ຂ້ອຍບໍ່ສົນ

Careful!
la-wáng — ລະວັງ

to carry	ạo máa	ເອົາມາ

I'll carry it.
khàwy já ạo máa — ຂ້ອຍຈະເອົາມາ

CD	phaen síi-dịi	ແຜ່ນຊີດີ

to celebrate	sá-lăwng	ສະຫລອງ
cemetery	paa sâa	ປ່າຊ້າ
certificate	bại yang-yéun	ໃບຢັ້ງຢືນ
certain (sure)	nae náwn	ແນ່ນອນ

Are you certain?
jâo nae jại baw — ເຈົ້າແນ່ໃຈບໍ່

chair	tang nang	ຕັ່ງນັ່ງ
chance	ọh-kàat	ໂອກາດ
by chance	dọhy bạng ọen	ໂດຍບັງເອີນ
change (money)	ngóen nâwy	ເງິນນ້ອຍ
cheap	thèuk	ຖືກ
cheese	nóei	ເນີຍ
chemist	phùu khăai yáa	ຜູ້ຂາຍຢາ
child	dék nâwy	ເດັກນ້ອຍ
chocolate	khào-nŏm sóh-kọh-laet	ເຂົ້າໜົມໂຊໂກແລັດ
to choose	lêuak	ເລືອກ
church	bòht khlit	ໂບດຄລິດ
cigarettes	yáa sùup	ຢາສູບ
cinema	hóng hûup ngáo	ໂຮງຮູບເງົາ
city	méuang	ເມືອງ
city centre	jại káang méuang	ໃຈກາງເມືອງ
clean (adj)	khwáam sá-àat	ຄວາມສະອາດ
close (nearby)	kâi	ໄກ້
to close	át/pít	ອັດ/ປິດ

It's closed.
pít lâew — ປິດແລ້ວ

clothing	kheuang nung	ເຄື່ອງນຸ່ງ
coin	ngóen lĭan	ເງິນຫລຽນ
cold (adj; climate)	năo	ໜາວ
cold (n)	khwáam năo	ຄວາມໜາວ

colour	sĭi	ສີ
to come	máa	ມາ
comfortable	sá-bạai	ສະບາຍ
communism	la-bàwp kháwm-múu-nit	ລະບອບຄອມມູນິດ
company (business)	bọw-li-sat	ບໍລິສັດ
complex (adj)	nyùng nyĕuang	ຫຍຸ້ງເຫຍືອງ
condom	thŏng yáang á-náa-mái	ຖົງຢາງອະນາໄມ
to confirm	yéun yán	ຢືນຢັນ

Congratulations!
sóm sóei ຊົມເຊີຍ

constipation	nyeung thâwng	ຍື່ງທ້ອງ
consulate	kọng-sŭun	ກົງສູນ
contact lens	waen sai kâew tạa	ແວ່ນໃສ່ແກ້ວຕາ
contagious	pha-nyâat tít-taw	ພະຍາດຕິດຕໍ່
contraceptive	sing khúm kạm-nôet	ສິ່ງຄຸມກຳເນີດ
conversation	kạan sŏn-tha-náa	ການສົນທະນາ
to cook	taeng kịn	ແຕ່ງກິນ
corner (of a room)	jạe hâwng	ແຈຫ້ອງ
corner (of a street)	tháang nyâek	ທາງແຍກ
at/on the corner	yuu tháang nyâek	ຢູ່ທາງແຍກ
corrupt (adj)	kịn sĭn bọn	ກິນສິນບົນ
corruption	kạan kịn sĭn bọn	ການກິນສິນບົນ
cost	láa-kháa	ລາຄາ
to cost	míi láa-kháa	ມີລາຄາ

It costs ...
mán míi láa-kháa ... ມັນມີລາຄາ ...

How much does it cost?
láa-kháa thao dại ລາຄາເທົ່າໃດ

to cough	ại	ໄອ
to count	nap	ນັບ

crazy	bâa	ບ້າ
credit card	bát khréh-dit	ບັດຄເຣດິດ
crop	phŏn-la-pùuk	ຜົນລະປູກ
cross (angry)	khîat khâen	ຄຽດແຄ້ນ
customs office	hàwng-kạan pháa-sĭi ạa-kạwn	ຫ້ອງການພາສີອາກອນ
to cut	tát	ຕັດ
to cycle	khii lot thìip	ຂີ່ລົດຖີບ

D

dad	phaw	ພໍ່
daily	pá-jạm wán	ປະຈຳວັນ
damp	jêun	ຈື້ນ
to dance	fâwn	ຟ້ອນ
dangerous	ạn-ta-láai	ອັນຕະລາຍ
dark	mêut	ມືດ
date (time)	wán thíi	ວັນທີ
date of birth	wán kòet	ວັນເກີດ
dawn	ạa-lún	ອາລຸນ
day	kạang wén	ກາງເວັນ
dead	tạai lâew	ຕາຍແລ້ວ
deaf	hŭu nùak	ຫູໜວກ
death	khwáam tạai	ຄວາມຕາຍ
to decide	tát sĭn jại	ຕັດສິນໃຈ
decision	kạan tát sĭn jại	ການຕັດສິນໃຈ
delay	jó	ໂຈະ
delicious	sâep	ແຊບ
delightful	muan seun	ມ່ວນຊື່ນ
democracy	pá-sáa-thi-pá-tại	ປະຊາທິປະໄຕ
demonstration (protest)	kạan dọen khá-bụan	ການເດີນຂະບວນ

to depart (leave)	àwk	ອອກ

The flight departs at ...
thìaw bịn àwk ... ຖ້ຽວບິນອອກ ...

What time does it leave?
àwk ják móhng ອອກຈັກໂມງ

department store	hâan sap-pha-sǐn-khâa	ຮ້ານຊັບພະສິນຄ້າ
departure	kạan àwk	ການອອກ
to destroy	thám láai	ທຳລາຍ
development	kạan phat-tha-náa	ການພັດທະນາ
diabetes	lôhk bạo-wǎan	ໂລກເບົາຫວານ
dictionary	pêum wat-já-náa-nu-kọm	ປື້ມວັດຈະນານຸກົມ
different	tàek-taang	ແຕກຕ່າງ
difficult	nyàak	ຫຍາກ

It's difficult.
nyùng nyàak ຫຍຸ້ງຫຍາກ

dinner	ạa-hǎan láeng	ອາຫານແລງ
direct	dọhy kọng	ໂດຍກົງ
direction (adv)	thit tháang	ທິດທາງ
dirt	dịn	ດິນ
dirty	pêuan	ເປື້ອນ
disabled person	khón phi-kạan	ຄົນພິການ
discount	lut láa-kháa	ລຸດລາຄາ
discrimination	kạan jạm-nâek	ການຈຳແນກ
disinfectant	yáa khàa sêua	ຢາຂ້າເຊື້ອ
distant	kại	ໄກ
to do	het	ເຮັດ

I'll do it.
khàwy síi het ຂ້ອຍຊິເຮັດ

Can you do that?
jâo het dâi baw ເຈົ້າເຮັດໄດ້ບໍ່

Don't do it.
yáa het — ຢ່າເຮັດ

doctor	thaan măw	ທ່ານໝໍ
dog	măa	ໝາ
doll	hun	ຮຸ່ນ
door	pá-tụu	ປະຕູ
double	khuu	ຄູ່
double bed	tịang khuu	ຕຽງຄູ່
double room	hàwng khuu	ຫ້ອງຄູ່
down	lum	ລຸ່ມ
downtown	kạang méuang	ກາງເມືອງ
dream	khwáam făn	ຄວາມຝັນ
to dream	făn	ຝັນ
to dress	nung	ໜຸ່ງ
dried	hàeng	ແຫ້ງ
drink	kheuang deum	ເຄື່ອງດື່ມ
to drink	deum	ດື່ມ

I don't drink spirits.
khàwy baw kịn lào — ຂ້ອຍບໍ່ກິນເຫຼົ້າ

Do you drink beer?
jâo kịn bịa baw — ເຈົ້າກິນເບຍບໍ່

drinkable	pẹn tạa deum	ເປັນຕາດື່ມ
drinkable water	nâm deum	ນ້ຳດື່ມ
to drive	kháp	ຂັບ (ລົດ)
drivers licence	bại á-nu-nyâat kháp-khii	ໃບອະນຸຍາດຂັບຂີ່
drugs (illegal)	yáa sèhp tít	ຢາເສບຕິດ
drunk (inebriated)	máo lào	ເມົາເຫຼົ້າ
dry (adj)	hàeng	ແຫ້ງ
during	la-waang	ລະຫວ່າງ
dust	khìi fun	ຂີ້ຝຸ່ນ

E

each	tae-la	ແຕ່ລະ
early	tae sâo	ແຕ່ເຊົ້າ
to earn	dâi	ໄດ້
earnings	láai hap	ລາຍຮັບ
Earth	nuay lôhk	ໜ່ວຍໂລກ
earthquake	phaen-dịn wăi	ແຜ່ນດິນໄຫວ
east	thit tạa-wén àwk	ທິດຕາເວັນອອກ
easy	ngaai	ງ່າຍ
to eat	kịn	ກິນ
economical	pá-yat	ປະຢັດ
economics	sèht-thá-sàat	ເສດຖະສາດ
economy	sèht-thá-kít	ເສດຖະກິດ
economy (thrift)	kạan pá-yat	ການປະຢັດ
education	kạan séuk-săa	ການສຶກສາ
elections	kạan lêuak tâng	ການເລືອກຕັ້ງ
electricity	fái fâa	ໄຟຟ້າ
elevator (lift)	lip (khân dại fái fâa)	ລິບ (ຂັ້ນໄດໄຟຟ້າ)
email	ị-máew	ອີແມວ
embassy	sá-thăan thûut	ສະຖານທູດ
emergency exit	tháang àwk súk sŏen	ທາງອອກສຸກເສີນ
employer	náai jâang	ນາຍຈ້າງ
empty	pao	ເປົ່າ
end	jóp	ຈົບ
energy	pha-láng-ngáan	ພະລັງງານ
English	pháa-săa ạng-kít	ພາສາອັງກິດ
to enjoy (oneself)	muan	ມ່ວນ
enough	phaw	ພໍ
to enter	khào	ເຂົ້າ
entrance	tháang khào	ທາງເຂົ້າ
entry	kạan-khào	ການເຂົ້າ

environment	sing wâet-lâwm	ສິ່ງແວດລ້ອມ
equal (adj)	thao káp	ເທົ່າກັບ
European (person)	khón yúu-lôhp	ຄົນຢູໂລບ
evening	tąwn khám	ຕອນຄ່ຳ
event	ngáan thêht-sá-kąan	ງານເທດສະການ
every	thuk-thuk/tae-la	ທຸກໆ/ແຕ່ລະ
every day	thuk wán	ທຸກວັນ
everyone	thuk khón	ທຸກຄົນ
everything	thuk yaang	ທຸກຢ່າງ
example	tųa yaang	ຕົວຢ່າງ
for example	yok tųa yaang	ຍົກຕົວຢ່າງ
to exchange	lâek pian	ແລກປ່ຽນ

Excuse me.
khăw thôht ຂໍໂທດ

exhausted	meuay	ເໝື່ອຍ
exhibition	wáang sá-dąeng	ວາງສະແດງ
exile	phùu theuk néh-la-thêht	ຜູ້ຖືກເນລະເທດ
to exile	néh-la-thêht	ເນລະເທດ
exit	tháang àwk	ທາງອອກ
expensive	pháeng	ແພງ
experience	pá-sóp-kąan	ປະສົບການ
export	sĭn-khâa song àwk	ສິນຄ້າສົ່ງອອກ
to export	song àwk sĭn-khâa	ສົ່ງອອກສິນຄ້າ
eye	tąa	ຕາ

F

false (wrong)	phít	ຜິດ
false (fake)	pąwm	ປອມ
family	khâwp khúa	ຄອບຄົວ
fan (cooling)	phat lóm	ພັດລົມ

F

fan (sports)	khăa khĭa	ຂາເຊຍ
far	kại	ໄກ
farm	bawn phá-lit ká-sí-kạm	ບ່ອນຜະລິດກະສິກຳ
fast (adj)	wái	ໄວ
to fast	ngot kịn ạa-hăan	ງົດກິນອາຫານ
fat (adj)	tûi	ຕຸ້ຍ
fat	khăi mán	ໄຂມັນ
father	phaw	ພໍ່
fault	khwáam phít phâat	ຄວາມຜິດພາດ

It's my fault.
khwáam phít khăwng khàwy ຄວາມຜິດຂອງຂ້ອຍ

fear	khwáam yâan	ຄວາມຢ້ານ
fee	láa-kháa	ລາຄາ
to feel	hûu-séuk	ຮູ້ສຶກ
feeling	khwáam-hûu-séuk	ຄວາມຮູ້ສຶກ
ferry	héua dọhy-săan	ເຮືອໂດຍສານ
festival	ngáan bụn	ງານບຸນ
fever	khài	ໄຂ້
few	nàwy	ໜ້ອຍ
a few	nàwy dịaw	ໜ້ອຍດຽວ
fiance(e)	khuu màn	ຄູ່ໝັ້ນ
film (movie)	hûup ngáo	ຮູບເງົາ
film (roll of)	fím thaai hûup	ຟິມຖ່າຍຮູບ
filtered (water)	nâm kạwng	ນ້ຳ ກອງ
fine (penalty)	páp măi	ປັບໃໝ
fire	fái	ໄຟ
firewood	féun	ຟືນ
first	thii neung	ທີ່ໜຶ່ງ
fish	pạa	ປາ
flag	thúng	ທຸງ

DICTIONARY

flashlight (torch)	fái sǎai	ໄຟສາຍ
flight	thìaw bịn	ຖ້ຽວບິນ
flood	ú-thok-ká-phái	ອຸທົກກະໄພ
floor	phêun	ພື້ນ
on the floor	yuu phêun	ຢູ່ພື້ນ
flower(s)	dàwk mâi	ດອກໄມ້
to follow	tạam	ຕາມ

Follow me!
tạam khàwy — ຕາມຂ້ອຍ

food	ạa-hǎan	ອາຫານ
food poisoning	ạa-hǎan pẹn phít	ອາຫານເປັນພິດ
football (soccer)	bạan-té	ບານເຕະ
foreign	taang pá-thêht	ຕ່າງປະເທດ
foreigner	khón taang pá-thêht	ຄົນຕ່າງປະເທດ
forever	tá-làwt kạan	ຕະຫລອດການ
to forget	léum	ລືມ

I forgot.
khàwy léum — ຂ້ອຍລືມ

to forgive	hài ạ-phái	ໃຫ້ອະໄພ
formal	tháang kạan	ທາງການ
fragile	kheuang tàek ngaai	ເຄື່ອງແຕກງ່າຍ
free (gratis)	hài lâa	ໃຫ້ລ້າ
free (not bound)	ít-sá-la	ອິດສະລະ
to freeze	sae khǎeng	ແຊ່ແຂງ
fresh	sót	ສົດ
friend	pheuan	ເພື່ອນ
friendly	pheuan mit	ເພື່ອນມິດ
full	tẹm	ເຕັມ
fun	muan	ມ່ວນ
funny	tá-lók	ຕະຫຼົກ

G

game	kạan lìin	ການຫລິ້ນ
garbage	khìi yèua	ຂີ້ເຫຍື້ອ
garden	sŭan	ສວນ
gas (cooking)	ạai kàet	ອາຍແກັສ
gas (petrol)	nâm-mán àet-sáng	ນ້ຳມັນແອັດຊັງ
gate	pá-tụu	ປະຕູ
generous	êua-fêua	ເອື້ອເຟື້ອ
gift	khăwng khwăn	ຂອງຂວັນ
girl	dék nyíng	ເດັກຍິງ
girlfriend	fáen (nyíng)	ແຟນ(ຍິງ)
to give	ạo hâi	ເອົາໃຫ້

Give me ...
ạo hâi dae ... ເອົາໃຫ້ແດ່ ...

I'll give you ...
já ạo hâi jâo ... ຈະເອົາໃຫ້ເຈົ້າ ...

glass (drinking)	jàwk	ຈອກ
glasses (spectacles)	waen tạa	ແວ່ນຕາ
to go (on foot)	pại (nyaang)	ໄປ (ຍ່າງ)

I'm going to ... (do something)
khàwy já ... ຂ້ອຍຈະ ...

I'm going to ... (somewhere)
khàwy já pại ... ຂ້ອຍຈະໄປ ...

Are you going there?
jâo sii pại hàn baw ເຈົ້າຊິໄປຫັ້ນບໍ່

God	pha-jâo	ພະເຈົ້າ
good	dịi	ດີ
government	lat-thá-bạan	ລັດຖະບານ
greedy	mak dâi	ມັກໄດ້

to grow (increase)	khá-nyăai	ຂະຫຍາຍ
to grow (produce)	pùuk	ປູກ
to guess	dạo	ເດົາ
guide	pha-nak-ngạan nám thiaw	ພະນັກງານນຳທ່ຽວ
guidebook	pêum nám thiaw	ປື້ມນຳທ່ຽວ
guilty	ká-thám phít	ກະທຳຜິດ
guitar	kí-tạa	ກີຕາ

H

hair	phŏm	ຜົມ
hairdresser	saang sŏem sŭay	ຊ່າງເສີມສວຍ
half	khoeng	ເຄິ່ງ
handbag	ká-pạo hìu	ກະເປົາຫິ້ວ
handicapped person	khón phi-kạan	ຄົນພິການ
handicrafts	hát-thá-kạm	ຫັດຖະກຳ
handsome	ngáam	ງາມ
happy	dịi-jại	ດີໃຈ

Happy Birthday!
súk-săn wán kòet — ສຸກສັນວັນເກີດ

hard (difficult)	nyàak	ຫຍາກ
hard (not soft)	khăeng	ແຂງ
to hate	sáng	ຊັງ
to have	míi	ມີ

I have ...
khàwy míi ... — ຂ້ອຍມີ ...

You have ...
jào míi ... — ເຈົ້າມີ ...

Do you have ...?
jâo míi ... baw — ເຈົ້າມີ ... ບໍ່

he	láo	ລາວ
health	sú-khá-phâap	ສຸຂະພາບ
health centre	sŭun á-náa-mái	ສູນອະນາໄມ
to hear	dâi-nyín	ໄດ້ຍິນ
heat	khwáam hâwn	ຄວາມຮ້ອນ
heater	kheuang het hài un	ເຄື່ອງເຮັດໃຫ້ອຸ່ນ
heavy	nák	ໜັກ
hello	sá-bạai dịi	ສະບາຍດີ
help	khwáam suay lĕua	ຄວາມຊ່ວຍເຫຼືອ
to help	suay	ຊ່ວຍ

Can I help (you)?
míi nyăng hài suay baw — ມີຫຍັງໃຫ້ຊ່ວຍບໍ່

Help!
sûay dae — ຊ່ວຍແດ່

here	yuu nîi	ຢູ່ນີ້
high	sŭung	ສູງ
hill	phúu	ພູ
to hire (someone)	jâang	ຈ້າງ

I'd like to hire him.
khàwy yàak jâang láo — ຂ້ອຍຢາກຈ້າງລາວ

to hire (rent)	sao	ເຊົ່າ

I'd like to hire it.
khàwy yàak sao — ຂ້ອຍຢາກເຊົ່າ

holiday (religious)	wán bụn	ວັນບຸນ
holiday (vacation)	wán phak wîak	ວັນພັກວຽກ
on holiday	pại thiaw	ໄປທ່ຽວ
school holidays	wán phak hían	ວັນພັກຮຽນ
holy	sák-sít	ສັກສິດ
home	héuan	ເຮືອນ
homeland	ma-tú-phúum	ມະຕຸພູມ

homosexual (adj)	mak phêht diaw-kan	ມັກເພດດຽວກັນ
homosexual	khón mak phêht diaw-kan	ຄົນມັກເພດດຽວກັນ
honest	seu-sát	ຊື່ສັດ
hope	khwáam wăng	ຄວາມຫວັງ
to hope	wăng	ຫວັງ
hospital	hóhng măw	ໂຮງໝໍ
hospitality	kaan tâwn hap	ການຕ້ອນຮັບ
hot	hâwn	ຮ້ອນ
hot (weather)	aa-kàat hâwn	ອາກາດຮ້ອນ
hot (spicy)	phét	ເຜັດ
hotel	hóhng háem	ໂຮງແຮມ
hotel room	hàwng phak hóhng háem	ຫ້ອງພັກໂຮງແຮມ
house	héuan	ເຮືອນ
housework	wîak heuan	ວຽກເຮືອນ
how	náew-dai	ແນວໃດ

How do I get to ...?
khàwy já pai hâwt ... dâi náew-dai
ຂ້ອຍຈະໄປຮອດ ... ໄດ້ແນວໃດ

How are you?
jâo sá-baai dii baw ...
ເຈົ້າສະບາຍດີບໍ່ ...

How much is/are ...?
láa-kháa thao dai ...
ລາຄາເທົ່າໃດ ...

human	ma-nut	ມະນຸດ
hungry	hĭu khào	ຫິວເຂົ້າ

I'm hungry.
khàwy hĭu khào
ຂ້ອຍຫິວເຂົ້າ

Are you hungry?
jâo hĭu khào baw
ເຈົ້າຫິວເຂົ້າບໍ່

to hurry	fâo	ຟ້າວ
I'm in a hurry.		
khàwy fâo		ຂ້ອຍຟ້າວ
to hurt	jép	ເຈັບ
My ... hurts.		
khàwy jép ...		ຂ້ອຍເຈັບ ...
husband	phŭa	ຜົວ

I

I	khàwy	ຂ້ອຍ
ice	nâm kâwn	ນ້ຳກ້ອນ
with ice	sai nâm kâwn	ໃສ່ນ້ຳກ້ອນ
without ice	baw sai nâm kâwn	ບໍ່ໃສ່ນ້ຳກ້ອນ
ice cream	ká-láen	ກະແລັມ
icon	ọa-nu-săwn	ອານຸສອນ
idea	náew khwáam khít	ແນວຄວາມຄິດ
identification	bát pá-jạm tụa	ບັດປະຈຳຕົວ
if	thàa waa	ຖ້າວ່າ
ill	khài	ໄຂ້
illegal	phít kót-măai	ຜິດກົດໝາຍ
imagination	jín-tá-náa-kạan	ຈິນຕະນາການ
imitation	khăwng pạwm	ຂອງປອມ
immediately	thán thíi	ທັນທີ
import	sĭn khâa khăa khào	ສິນຄ້າຂາເຂົ້າ
to import	kạan nám khào	ການນຳເຂົ້າ
important	săm-khán	ສຳຄັນ
impossible	pẹn pại baw dâi	ເປັນໄປບໍ່ໄດ້
imprisonment	tít khuk	ຕິດຄຸກ
in	nái	ໃນ
included	pá-kàwp dûay	ປະກອບດ້ວຍ
inconvenient	baw sá-dùak	ບໍ່ສະດວກ
industry	út-săa-há-kạm	ອຸດສາຫະກຳ

infectious	tít sêua	ຕິດເຊື້ອ
infection	kạan tít sêua	ການຕິດເຊື້ອ
informal	baw pẹn tháang kạan	ບໍ່ເປັນທາງການ
information	khàw múun	ຂໍ້ມູນ
injection	kạan sák yáa	ການສັກຢາ
injury	bàat jép	ບາດເຈັບ
insect repellent	yáa kạn máeng mâi	ຢາກັນແມງໄມ້
inside	pháai nái	ພາຍໃນ
insurance	pá-kạn phái	ປະກັນໄພ
to insure	pá-kạn	ປະກັນ

It's insured.
pá-kạn lâew ປະກັນແລ້ວ

intelligent	sá-làat	ສະຫລາດ
interested	sǒn-jại	ສົນໃຈ
interesting	pẹn tạa sǒn-jại	ເປັນຕາສົນໃຈ
international	la-waang sâat	ລະຫວ່າງຊາດ
Internet	ịn-tọe-naet	ອິນເຕີແນັດ
Internet cafe	ịn-tọe-naet kạa-féh	ອິນເຕີແນັດກາເຟ
invitation	bát sóen	ບັດເຊີນ

J

jail	khuk	ຄຸກ
jazz	tọn-tịi jàet	ດົນຕີແຈສ
jeans	sòng yíin	ສົ້ງຢີນ
jewellery	kheuang pá-dáp	ເຄື່ອງປະດັບ
job	wîak	ວຽກ
joke	khwáam yâwk	ຄວາມຢອກ

I'm joking.
khàwy wâo yâwk ຂ້ອຍເວົ້າຢອກ

journey	dọen tháang	ເດີນທາງ
juice (fruit)	nâm màak mâi	ນ້ຳໝາກໄມ້
justice	khwáam nyu-tí-thám	ຄວາມຍຸຕິທຳ

K		
key	ká-jąe	ກະແຈ
to kill	khàa	ຂ້າ
kind	jąi dįi	ໃຈດີ
king	jâo síi-wit	ເຈົ້າຊີວິດ
kiss	kąan jùup	ການຈູບ
to kiss	jùup	ຈູບ
knapsack	bąa-lóh	ບາໂລ
to know (a person)	hûu-ják	ຮູ້ຈັກ

I know him.
khàwy hûu-ják láo ຂ້ອຍຮູ້ຈັກລາວ

to know (something)	hûu	ຮູ້
L		
lake	năwng	ໜອງ
land	phaen dįn	ແຜ່ນດິນ
landslide	dįn thá-lom	ດິນຖະຫລົ່ມ
language	pháa-săa	ພາສາ
large	kwâang/nyai	ກ້ວາງ/ໃຫຍ່
last (in a series)	sút-thâai	ສຸດທ້າຍ
last (as in 'last week')	kawn	ກ່ອນ
late	sâa	ຊ້າ
to be late	máa sâa	ມາຊ້າ

I'm late!
khàwy máa sâa ຂ້ອຍມາຊ້າ

later	tąwn lăng	ຕອນຫລັງ
to laugh	hŭa	ຫົວ

Don't laugh!
yaa hŭa ຢ່າຫົວ

laundry (washing)	sak kheuang	ຊັກເຄື່ອງ

laundry (place)	hóhng sak kheuang	ໂຮງຊັກເຄື່ອງ
law	kót-măai	ກົດໝາຍ
lawyer	nak kót-măai	ນັກກົດໝາຍ
lazy	khâan	ຄ້ານ
to learn	hían	ຮຽນ

I want to learn Lao.
khàwy yàak hían pháa-săa láo — ຂ້ອຍຢາກຮຽນພາສາລາວ

to leave (depart)	àwk; àwk jàak	ອອກ; ອອກຈາກ

The flight leaves at ...
thìaw bịn àwk wéh-láa ... — ຖ້ຽວບິນອອກເວລາ ...

What time does the bus leave?
lot méh àwk ják móhng — ລົດເມອອກຈັກໂມງ

We're leaving for Vientiane tonight.
khéun nîi phûak háo já àwk pại wíeng jạn — ຄືນນີ້ພວກເຮົາຈະ ອອກໄປວຽງຈັນ

to leave (behind)	pá-wâi	ປະໄວ້
lecturer	wi-tha-nyáa-kạwn	ວິທະຍາກອນ
left (not right)	bêuang sâi	ເບື້ອງຊ້າຍ
on/to the left	tháang sâi	ທາງຊ້າຍ
legal	thèuk kót-măai	ຖືກກົດໝາຍ
less	nàwy-kwaa	ໜ້ອຍກ່ວາ
letter	jót-măai	ຈົດໝາຍ
liar	khón khìi tua	ຄົນຂີ້ຕົວະ
lice	hăo	ເຫົາ
life	síi-wit	ຊີວິດ
lift (elevator)	lip (khân dại fái fâa)	ລິບ (ຂັ້ນໄດໄຟຟ້າ)
light (not heavy)	bạo	ເບົາ
light	fái	ໄຟ
lighter (cigarette)	káp fái	ກັບໄຟ
like (similar)	khéu	ຄື

L

to like	mak	ມັກ
I like ... khàwy mak ...		ຂ້ອຍມັກ ...
Do you like ...? jâo mak ... baw		ເຈົ້າມັກ ... ບໍ່
line	sèn seu	ເສັ້ນຊື່
to listen	fáng	ຟັງ
Listen to me. fáng khàwy		ຟັງຂ້ອຍ
little (dimension)	nàwy	ໜ້ອຍ
little (quantity)	nàwy	ໜ້ອຍ
to live	ąa-săi yuu	ອາໄສຢູ່
I live in ... khàwy yuu ...		ຂ້ອຍຢູ່ ...
Where do you live? jâo yuu săi		ເຈົ້າຢູ່ໃສ
local	thâwng thin	ທ້ອງຖິ່ນ
lock	lái/kąwn	ໄລ/ກອນ
long	nyáo	ຍາວ
long ago	tae dǫn	ແຕ່ດົນ
to look	boeng	ເບິ່ງ
to look for	sâwk hăa	ຊອກຫາ
to lose	sĭa	ເສຍ
I've lost my money. khàwy het ngóen sĭa		ຂ້ອຍເຮັດເງິນເສຍ
to lose (one's way)	lŏng tháang	ຫຼົງທາງ
I'm lost. khàwy lŏng tháang		ຂ້ອຍຫລົງທາງ
lost (adj, things)	sĭa hăai	ເສຍຫາຍ
loud	dąng	ດັງ

love	khwáam hak	ຄວາມຮັກ
to love (be fond of)	mak	ມັກ
to love (relationships)	hak	ຮັກ

I love you.
khàwy hak jâo — ຂ້ອຍຮັກເຈົ້າ

luck	sôhk	ໂຊກ
lucky	míi sôhk	ມີໂຊກ
luggage	ká-pąo	ກະເປົາ
lunch	ąa-hăan thiang	ອາຫານທ່ຽງ

M

machine	kheuang ják	ເຄື່ອງຈັກ
mad (crazy)	bâa	ບ້າ
made (of)	phá-lit dọhy	ຜະລິດໂດຍ
mail	jot-măai	ຈົດໝາຍ
main	săm-khán	ສຳຄັນ
majority	suan nyai	ສ່ວນໃຫຍ່
to make	het	ເຮັດ

Did you make it?
jâo het baw — ເຈົ້າເຮັດບໍ່

man	phùu sáai	ຜູ້ຊາຍ
many	lăai	ຫຼາຍ
map	phăen-thii	ແຜນທີ່
market	ta-làat	ຕະຫລາດ
at the market	yuu ta-làat	ຢູ່ຕະຫລາດ
marriage	kąan taeng-ngáan	ການແຕ່ງງານ
to marry	taeng-ngáan	ແຕ່ງງານ

I'm married.
khàwy taeng-ngáan lâew — ຂ້ອຍແຕ່ງງານແລ້ວ

massage	nûat	ນວດ

matches	káp-khìit	ກັບຂີດ
maybe	bạang thii	ບາງທີ
medicine	yáa	ຢາ
to meet (someone)	phop	ພົບ
I'll meet you. khàwy já phop jâo		ຂ້ອຍຈະພົບເຈົ້າ
to meet (each other)	phop kạn	ພົບກັນ
Let's meet! phop kạn thaw		ພົບກັນເທາະ
menu	láai-kạan ạa-hǎan	ລາຍການອາຫານ
message	khàw-khwáam	ຂໍ້ຄວາມ
milk	nâm nóm	ນ້ຳນົມ
million	lâan	ລ້ານ
mind	jít jại	ຈິດໃຈ
to mind (to object)	baw hěn dịi	ບໍ່ເຫັນດີ
Do you mind ...? ... pẹn nyǎng baw		... ເປັນຫຍັງບໍ່
Never mind! baw pẹn nyǎng		ບໍ່ເປັນຫຍັງ
mineral water	nâm háe thâat	ນ້ຳແຮທາດ
minute	náa-thii	ນາທີ
to miss (someone)	khit hâwt	ຄິດຮອດ
mistake	khwáam phít	ຄວາມຜິດ
to make a mistake	het phít	ເຮັດຜິດ
You've made a mistake. jâo het phít		ເຈົ້າເຮັດຜິດ
to mix	pá-sǒm kạn	ປະສົມກັນ
modern	thán sá-mǎi	ທັນສະໄໝ
money	ngóen	ເງິນ
month	dẹuan	ເດືອນ

monument	á-nu-săa-wa-líi	ອະນຸສາວະລີ
more (of something)	ìik	ອີກ
morning	tạwn sâo	ຕອນເຊົ້າ
mountain	phúu dạwy	ພູດອຍ
mountain-climbing	khèun phúu	ຂຶ້ນພູ
mother	mae	ແມ່
movie	hûup ngáo	ຮູບເງົາ

Let's see a movie.
pại boeng hûup ngáo ໄປເບິ່ງຮູບເງົາ

museum	phi-phit-tha-phán	ພິພິດທະພັນ
music	dọn-tịi	ດົນຕີ
musician	nak-dọn-tịi	ນັກດົນຕີ

N

name	seu	ຊື່

My name is ...
khàwy seu ... ຂ້ອຍຊື່ ...

What's your name?
jâo seu nyăng ເຈົ້າຊື່ຫຍັງ

national park	sŭan út-thi-nyáan	ສວນອຸດທິຍານ
nature	thám-ma-sâat	ທຳມະຊາດ
near (prep)	kâi	ໄກ້
nearby	yuu kâi	ຢູ່ໄກ້
necessary	jạm-pẹn	ຈຳເປັນ
need	tâwng-kạan	ຕ້ອງການ

I need ...
khàwy tâwng-kạan ... ຂ້ອຍຕ້ອງການ ...

We need ...
háo tâwng-kạan ... ເຮົາຕ້ອງການ ...

neither ... nor	baw ... lěu	ບໍ່ ... ຫຼື
never	baw khóei	ບໍ່ເຄີຍ
new	mai	ໃໝ່
news	khao	ຂ່າວ
newspaper	năng-sěu phím	ໜັງສືພິມ
next	taw pại	ຕໍ່ໄປ
night	khám	ຄ່ຳ
no	baw	ບໍ່
noise	sĭang dạng	ສຽງດັງ
noisy	song sĭang dạng	ສົ່ງສຽງດັງ
north	nĕua	ເໜືອ
nothing	baw míi nyăng	ບໍ່ມີຫຍັງ
not yet	nyáng	ຍັງ

We aren't in Vientiane yet.
phûak háo nyáng baw
than hâwt wíeng jạn
ພວກເຮົາຍັງ
ບໍ່ທັນຮອດວຽງຈັນ

now	dịaw-nîi	ດຽວນີ້

O

obvious	thii hûu kạn dịi	ທີ່ຮູ້ກັນດີ
occupation	ạa-sîip	ອາຊີບ
ocean	ma-hăa-sá-mut	ມະຫາສະມຸດ
to offend	luang kọen	ລ່ວງເກີນ
to offer	ạo hài	ເອົາໃຫ້
office	hàwng kạan	ຫ້ອງການ
often	sá-mam sá-mŏe	ສະໝ່ຳສະເໝີ
oil (petroleum)	nâm-mán	ນ້ຳມັນ
oil (vegetable)	nâm-mán phêut	ນ້ຳມັນພືດ
OK	tók-lóng	ຕົກລົງ

old	kae/thâo	ແກ/ເຖົ້າ
Olympic Games	kí-láa ọh-láem-pík	ກິລາໂອແລມປິກ
on (location)	yuu thóeng	ຢູ່ເທິງ
on (a particular day)	thii	ທີ
once	theua dịaw	ເທື່ອດຽວ
once more	ìik theua neung	ອີກເທື່ອໜຶ່ງ
once (upon a time)	tae kawn	ແຕ່ກ່ອນ
one	neung	ໜຶ່ງ
one-way	thìaw dịaw	ຖ້ຽວດຽວ
only	thao-nân	ເທົ່ານັ້ນ
open (adj)	pòet	ເປີດ
opinion	khwáam khit-hěn	ຄວາມຄິດເຫັນ

In my opinion ...
tạam khwáam khit khàwy ... ຕາມຄວາມຄິດຂ້ອຍ...

opportunity	ọh-kàat	ໂອກາດ
opposite (adj)	tàek taang	ແຕກຕ່າງ
opposite (prep)	kọng kạn khàam	ກົງກັນຂ້າມ
or	lěu	ຫຼື
order	khám-sang	ຄຳສັ່ງ
to order	sang	ສັ່ງ
ordinary	thám-ma-dạa	ທຳມະດາ
organisation	ọng-kạan ját tâng	ອົງການຈັດຕັ້ງ
to organise	ját	ຈັດ
original	tôn sá-báp	ຕົ້ນສະບັບ
other	eun	ອື່ນ
outside	tháang-nâwk	ທາງນອກ
over (prep)	yuu thóeng	ຢູ່ເທິງ
overnight	háem khéun	ແຮມຄືນ
overseas	taang pá-thêht	ຕ່າງປະເທດ

to owe	tít-nìi	ຕິດໜີ້

I owe you.
khàwy tít nìi jâo — ຂ້ອຍຕິດໜີ້ເຈົ້າ

You owe me.
jâo tít nìi khàwy — ເຈົ້າຕິດໜີ້ຂ້ອຍ

owner	jâo khǎwng	ເຈົ້າຂອງ

P

pack (of cigarettes)	sáwng (yáa sùup)	ຊອງ (ຢາສູບ)
package	haw	ຫໍ່
packet	sáwng	ຊອງ
padlock	ká-jạe	ກະແຈ
painful	jép	ເຈັບ
painkillers	yáa kâe pùat	ຢາແກ້ປວດ
painting	hûup tâem	ຮູບແຕ້ມ
pair	khuu	ຄູ່
palace	wáng	ວັງ
paper	jîa	ເຈ້ຍ
parcel	kheuang fàak	ເຄື່ອງຝາກ
parents	phaw mae	ພໍ່ແມ່
park	sǔan sǎa-tháa-la-na	ສວນສາທາລະນະ
parliament	sá-pháa phùu tháen	ສະພາຜູ້ແທນ
part	phâak suan	ພາກສ່ວນ
to participate	míi suan huam	ມີສ່ວນຮ່ວມ
participation	kạan khào huam	ການເຂົ້າຮ່ວມ
party (fiesta)	ngáan pạa-tịi	ງານປາຕີ
party (political)	phak kạan méuang	ພັກການເມືອງ
passenger	phùu dọhy-sǎan	ຜູ້ໂດຍສານ
passport	nǎng-sěu phaan dạen	ໜັງສືຜ່ານແດນ·
path	tháang nyaang	ທາງຍ່າງ

to pay	jaai	จ่าย
peace	săn-tí-phâap	สันติพาบ
people (crowd)	fŭung són	ฝูງຊົນ
people (nation)	pá-sáa-són	ປະຊາຊົນ
perfect (adj)	sŏm-bụun	ສົມບູນ
permanent	thăa-wáwn	ຖາວອນ
permission	kạan á-nu-mat	ການອະນຸມັດ
with your permission	á-nu-mat jàak jâo	ອະນຸມັດຈາກເຈົ້າ
permit	bại á-nu-nyâat	ໃບອະນຸຍາດ
to permit	á-nu-nyâat	ອະນຸຍາດ
persecution	kạan lóng thôht	ການລົງໂທດ
person	khón	ຄົນ
personal	suan tụa	ສ່ວນຕົວ
personality	ní-săi	ນິໄສ
petrol	nâm-mán àet-sáng	ນ້ຳມັນແອັດຊັງ
pharmacy	hâan khăai yáa	ຮ້ານຂາຍຢາ
phone book	pêum thóh-la-sáp	ປຶ້ມໂທລະສັບ
photograph	hûup thaai	ຮູບຖ່າຍ
to photograph	thaai hûup	ຖ່າຍຮູບ

Can I take a photograph?
khàw thaai hûup dâi baw — ຂ້ອຍຖ່າຍຮູບໄດ້ບໍ່

piece	pìang	ປ່ຽງ
place	bawn	ບ່ອນ
plant	phêut	ພືດ
plate	jạan	ຈານ
play (theatre)	la-kháwn	ລະຄອນ
to play	lìn	ຫຼິ້ນ

Please.
ká-lu-náa — ກະລຸນາ

plenty	lǎai	ຫຼາຍ
poetry	ká-wíi	ກະວີ
to point (with one's finger)	sîi méu	ຊີ້ມື
police	tạm-lùat	ຕຳຫລວດ
politics	kạan-méuang	ການເມືອງ
pollution	món-la-phit	ມົນລະພິດ
pool (swimming)	sa láwy nâm	ສະລອຍນ້ຳ
poor	thuk-jọn	ທຸກຈົນ
port	thaa héua	ທ່າເຮືອ
positive (certain)	nae jại	ແນ່ໃຈ

I'm positive.
khàwy nae jại — ຂ້ອຍແນ່ໃຈ

postage stamp	sá-tạem	ສະແຕມ
postcard	bát pại-sá-níi	ບັດໄປສະນີ
post code	la-hát pại-sá-níi	ລະຫັດໄປສະນີ
post office	hàwng-kạan pại-sa-níi	ຫ້ອງການໄປສະນີ
pottery (items)	kheuang pân dịn phǎo	ເຄື່ອງປັ້ນດິນເຜົາ
pottery (place)	bawn phá-lit kheuang pân dịn phǎo	ບ່ອນຜະລິດເຄື່ອງ ປັ້ນດິນເຜົາ
poverty	khwáam thuk-jọn	ຄວາມທຸກຈົນ
power (strength)	pha-láng	ພະລັງ
power (political)	ạm-nâat	ອຳນາດ
practical	sing thii pẹn pại dâi	ສິ່ງທີ່ເປັນໄປໄດ້
prayer	khám á-thi-thǎan	ຄຳອະທິຖານ
to prefer	mák	ມັກ

I prefer ...
khàwy mák ... — ຂ້ອຍມັກ ...

pregnant	thěu pháa	ຖືພາ

present (now)	pá-jú-bạn	ປະຈຸບັນ
present (gift)	khǎwng khwǎn	ຂອງຂວັນ
president	pá-tháan pá-thêht	ປະທານປະເທດ
pretty	ngáam	ງາມ
prevent	pâwng-kạn	ປ້ອງກັນ
price	láa-kháa	ລາຄາ
priest	khún phaw	ຄຸນພໍ່
prime minister	náa-yok	ນາຍົກ
prison	khuk	ຄຸກ
prisoner	nak-thôht	ນັກໂທດ
private	èh-ká-són	ເອກະຊົນ
probably	àat-já	ອາດຈະ
problem	pạn-hǎa	ປັນຫາ
procession	khá-bụan	ຂະບວນ
to produce	phá-lit	ຜະລິດ
professional	méu ọa-sîip	ມືອາຊີບ
profit	kạm-lái	ກຳໄລ
promise	kạan sǎn-nyáa	ການສັນຍາ
to promise	sǎn-nyáa	ສັນຍາ
prostitute	sǒh-phéh-níi	ໂສເພນີ
to protect	pâwng-kạn	ປ້ອງກັນ
protest	kạan pá-thûang	ການປະທ້ວງ
to protest	pá-thûang	ປະທ້ວງ
public	khǎwng sǎa-tháa-la-na	ຂອງສາທາລະນະ
public (adj)	sǎa-tháa-la-na	ສາທາລະນະ
in public	bawn sǎa-tháa-la-na	ບ່ອນສາທາລະນະ
to pull	dẹung	ດຶງ
to push	nyûu	ຍູ້
to put	wáang/sai	ວາງ/ໃສ່

Q

quality	khún-na-phâap	ຄຸນນະພາບ
of good quality	khún-na-phâap dịi	ຄຸນນະພາບດີ
question	khám thăam	ຄຳຖາມ
queue	khíu/thăew	ຄິວ/ແຖວ
quick (adj)	wái	ໄວ
quickly	wái	ໄວ
quiet (adj)	ngîap	ງຽບ

R

race (contest)	kạan khaeng-khăn	ການແຂ່ງຂັນ
racist	khón jạm-nâek phĭu phán	ຄນຈຳແນກຜິວພັນ
radio	wi-tha-nyu	ວິທະຍຸ
railway	tháang lot fái	ທາງລົດໄຟ
by rail	dọhy lot fái	ໂດຍລົດໄຟ
rain	fŏn	ຝົນ

It's raining.
fŏn tók ຝົນຕົກ

rape	kha-dịi khom khĕun	ຄະດີຂົ່ມຂືນ
to rape	khom khĕun	ຂົ່ມຂືນ
rare (unusual)	hăa nyàak	ຫາຫຍາກ
raw	díp	ດິບ
razor blades	bại-mîit thăe	ໃບມີດແຖ
to read	aan	ອ່ານ
ready	phâwm lâew	ພ້ອມແລ້ວ
reason	săa-het	ສາເຫດ
receipt	bại hap ngóen	ໃບຮັບເງິນ
recently	ạa-dìit phaan pại baw dọn	ອາດີດຜ່ານໄປບໍ່ດົນ
to recommend	nae-nám	ແນະນຳ

refrigerator	tûu yén	ຕູ້ເຢັນ
refugee	óp-pha-nyop	ອົບພະຍົບ
refund	tháen khéun	ແທນຄືນ
refuse	khìi nyèua	ຂີ້ເຫຍື້ອ
to refuse	pá-tí-sèht	ປະຕິເສດ
region	khŏng-khèht	ຂົງເຂດ
registered letter	jót-măai long tha-bịan	ຈົດໝາຍລົງທະບຽນ
regulation	kót la-bìap	ກົດລະບຽບ
relationship	khwáam săm-phán	ຄວາມສຳພັນ
to relax	phak phawn	ພັກຜ່ອນ
religion	sàat-sá-náa	ສາສະນາ
to remember	jeu	ຈື່
remote	thu-la kạn-dạan	ທຸລະກັນດານ
rent	khaa sao	ຄ່າເຊົ່າ
to rent	sao	ເຊົ່າ
to repair	pạeng	ແປງ
to repeat	wâo mai	ເວົ້າໃໝ່

Please repeat that.
ká-lu-náa wâo mai ກະລຸນາເວົ້າໃໝ່

representative	tụa tháen	ຕົວແທນ
republic	săa-tháa-la-na-lat	ສາທາລະນະລັດ
reservation	kạan sang-jạwng	ການສັ່ງຈອງ
reserve	sá-ngŭan	ສະຫງວນ
to reserve	sang-jạwng	ສັ່ງຈອງ
respect	khwáam kháo-lop	ຄວາມເຄົາລົບ
to respect	kháo-lop	ເຄົາລົບ
responsibility	khwáam hap-phít-sâwp	ຄວາມຮັບຜິດຊອບ
rest (relaxation)	kạan phak-phawn	ການພັກຜ່ອນ
to rest	phak-phawn	ພັກຜ່ອນ
restaurant	hâan ạa-hăan	ຮ້ານອາຫານ

to return	káp	ກັບ

We'll return on ...
phûak háo ja káp ... ພວກເຮົາຈະກັບ ...

return ticket	pîi pại-káp	ປີ້ໄປກັບ
rich	hang	ຮັ່ງ
right (not left)	bêuang khwăa	ເບື້ອງຂວາ
on/to the right	tháang khwăa	ທາງຂວາ
right (correct)	thèuk	ຖືກ

I'm right.
khàwy thèuk ຂ້ອຍຖືກ

risk	siang	ສ່ຽງ
river	mae nâm	ແມ່ນ້ຳ
road	tháang	ທາງ
robber	nak-pûn	ນັກປຸ້ນ
robbery	kạan pûn	ການປຸ້ນ
roof	lăng-kháa	ຫຼັງຄາ
room (general)	hàwng	ຫ້ອງ
room (hotel)	hàwng phak	ຫ້ອງພັກ
rope	sêuak	ເຊືອກ
round	wóng món	ວົງມົນ
rubbish	khìi nyèua	ຂີ້ເຫຍື້ອ
ruins	sàak sá-lak-hak-pháng	ສາກສະລັກຮັກພັງ
rule	la-bìap	ລະບຽບ

S

sad	sào	ເສົ້າ
safe (adj)	pàwt-phái	ປອດໄພ
safe	tûu sep	ຕູ້ເຊັບ
safely	dûay khwáam pàwt-phái	ດ້ວຍຄວາມປອດໄພ
safety	khwáam pàwt-phái	ຄວາມປອດໄພ
same	khéu-kạn	ຄືກັນ

to say	wâo	ເວົ້າ
I said ... khàwy dâi wâo ...		ຂ້ອຍໄດ້ເວົ້າ ...
Can you say that again? jâo wâo mai dâi baw		ເຈົ້າເວົ້າໃໝ່ໄດ້ບໍ່
scenery	thíu-that	ທິວທັດ
school	hóhng hían	ໂຮງຮຽນ
secret (adj)	lap	ລັບ
secret	khwáam lap	ຄວາມລັບ
to see	hĕn	ເຫັນ
I see. (understand) khàwy khào jại		ຂ້ອຍເຂົ້າໃຈ
I see (it). khàwy hĕn		ຂ້ອຍເຫັນ
selfish	hĕn kae tụa	ເຫັນແກ່ຕົວ
to sell	khăai	ຂາຍ
Do you sell ...? jâo khăai ... baw		ເຈົ້າຂາຍ ... ບໍ່
to send	song	ສົ່ງ
sentence (grammar)	pá-yòhk	ປະໂຫຍກ
serious	nák-năa	ໜັກໜາ
several	lăai	ຫຼາຍ
shade	hom	ຮົ່ມ
share	hùn	ຫຸ້ນ
to share	baeng kạn	ແບ່ງກັນ
she	láo	ລາວ
shoes	kòep	ເກີບ
shop	hâan khâa	ຮ້ານຄ້າ
short (length, duration)	sàn	ສັ້ນ
a short time ago	waang măw măw nîi	ຫວ່າງໝໍ່ໆນີ້
short (height)	tîa	ເຕັ້ຍ

shortage	khàat khŏen	ຂາດເຂີນ
to shout	hâwng	ຮ້ອງ
to show	sá-dąeng	ສະແດງ

Show me, please.
ąo hài khàwy boeng dae — ເອົາໃຫ້ຂ້ອຍເບິ່ງແດ່

shut (adj)	pít lâew	ປິດແລ້ວ
to shut	pít	ປິດ
shy	ąai	ອາຍ
sick	khài	ໄຂ້
sickness	lôhk	ໂລກ
sign	pâai	ປ້າຍ
signature	láai sén	ລາຍເຊັນ
similar	khâai khéu kąn	ຄ້າຍຄືກັນ
since (from that time)	tang tae	ຕັ້ງແຕ່
since (because)	neuang jàak waa	ເນື່ອງຈາກວ່າ
single (unmarried)	sòht	ໂສດ
sister	nâwng săo	ນ້ອງສາວ
to sit	nang	ນັ່ງ

Sit down.
nang lóng — ນັ່ງລົງ

situation	sá-phâap-kąan	ສະພາບການ
size	khá-nàat	ຂະໜາດ
sleep	kąan náwn	ການນອນ
to sleep	náwn	ນອນ

I'm asleep.
khàwy kąm-láng náwn — ຂ້ອຍກຳລັງນອນ

He's asleep.
láo náwn lap — ລາວນອນລັບ

Are you asleep?
jâo náwn lap baw — ເຈົ້ານອນລັບບໍ່

sleepy	hĭu náwn	ຫິວນອນ

I'm sleepy.
khàwy hĭu náwn ຂ້ອຍຫິວນອນ

slow	sâa	ຊ້າ
slowly	sâa	ຊ້າ
small	nâwy	ນ້ອຍ
smell	kin	ກິ່ນ
to smell	dọm	ດົມ
snow	hí-ma	ຫິມະ
soap	sá-bụu	ສະບູ
solid (adj)	năa nâen; khăeng	ໜາແໜ້ນ; ແຂງ
some	bạang	ບາງ
someone	bạang khón	ບາງຄົນ
something	bạang yaang	ບາງຢ່າງ
sometimes	bạang khâng	ບາງຄັ້ງ
son	lûuk sáai	ລູກຊາຍ
song	phéhng	ເພງ
so-so	thám-ma-dạa	ທຳມະດາ
soon	nái wái-wái nîi	ໃນໄວໆນີ້

Sorry!
khăw thôht ຂໍໂທດ

south	tâi	ໃຕ້
souvenir	khăwng khwăn	ຂອງຂວັນ
to speak	wâo	ເວົ້າ
special	phi-sèht	ພິເສດ
spirits (alcohol)	lào	ເຫຼົ້າ
sport	kí-láa	ກິລາ
spring (season)	la-dụu bạan mai	ລະດູບານໃໝ່
square	já-tú-lat	ຈະຕຸລັດ

S

stairway	khàn dại	ຂັ້ນໄດ
stamp	sá-tạem	ສະແຕມ
standard (adj)	mâat-tá-thăan	ມາດຕະຖານ
station (bus)	sá-thăa-níi (lot)	ສະຖານີ (ລົດ)
stay	kạan phak háem	ການພັກແຮມ
to stay	phak	ພັກ

I'll stay here for (two days).
khàwy já phak yuu nîi (săwng mêu) — ຂ້ອຍຈະພັກຢູ່ນີ້ (ສອງມື້)

to steal	lak	ລັກ

My money has been stolen.
ngóen khàwy thèuk lak — ເງິນຂ້ອຍຖືກລັກ

stop	bawn jàwt	ບ່ອນຈອດ
to stop	yut	ຢຸດ
storey	sân	ຊັ້ນ
ground floor	sân lum	ຊັ້ນລຸ່ມ
storm	pháa-nyu	ພາຍຸ
story	ni-tháan	ນິທານ
straight	seu	ຊື່
straight ahead	seu pại	ຊື່ໄປ
strange	pàek	ແປກ
stranger	khón pàek nàa	ຄົນແປກໜ້າ
street	thá-nŏn	ຖະໜົນ
on strike	pá-thûang	ປະທ້ວງ
strong	khăeng háeng	ແຂງແຮງ
student	nak-séuk-săa	ນັກສຶກສາ
stupid	ngoh	ໂງ່
suddenly	ká-than-hăn	ກະທັນຫັນ
suitcase	ká-pao	ກະເປົາ
summer	la-dụu hâwn	ລະດູຮ້ອນ
sun	tạa-wén	ຕາເວັນ

DICTIONARY

sure (certain)	nae jai	ແນ່ໃຈ

Are you sure?
jâo nae jai baw — ເຈົ້າແນ່ໃຈບໍ່

I'm sure.
khàwy nae jai — ຂ້ອຍແນ່ໃຈ

surname	náam sá-kun	ນາມສະກຸນ
surprise	pá-làat jai	ປະຫລາດໃຈ
sweet	wăan	ຫວານ
sweets (candy)	khào-nŏm	ເຂົ້າໜົມ
to swim	láwy nâm	ລອຍນ້ຳ

T

table	tó	ໂຕະ
to take	ao	ເອົາ

I'll take one.
khàwy já ao an neung — ຂ້ອຍຈະເອົາອັນໜຶ່ງ

Can I take this?
khàwy ao an nîi dâi baw — ຂ້ອຍເອົາອັນນີ້ໄດ້ບໍ່

to talk	wâo	ເວົ້າ
tall	sŭung	ສູງ
tasty	sâep	ແຊບ
tax	pháa-sĭi	ພາສີ
taxi	lot thaek-síi	ລົດແທັກຊີ
teacher	náai khúu	ນາຍຄູ
telephone	thóh-la-sáp	ໂທລະສັບ
to telephone	thóh-la-sáp	ໂທລະສັບ
telephone book	pêum thóh-la-sáp	ປື້ມໂທລະສັບ
temperature	un-na-phúum	ອຸນນະພູມ
tent	phàa tên	ຜ້າເຕັ້ນ

to thank	khăw khàwp jại	ຂໍຂອບໃຈ

Thank you.
khàwp jại ຂອບໃຈ

theatre	hóhng la-kháwn	ໂຮງລະຄອນ
there	yuu hàn	ຢູ່ຫັ້ນ
they	phûak khăo	ພວກເຂົາ
thick	năa	ໜາ
thief	jọhn	ໂຈນ
thin	bạang	ບາງ
to think	khit	ຄິດ
thirst	hĭw nâm	ຫິວນ້ຳ

I'm thirsty.
khàwy hĭw nâm ຂ້ອຍຫິວນ້ຳ

ticket	pîi	ປີ້
time	wéh-láa	ເວລາ

What time is it?
wéh-láa ják móhng ເວລາຈັກໂມງ

I don't have time.
khàwy baw míi wéh-láa ຂ້ອຍບໍ່ມີເວລາ

timetable	táa-láang wéh-láa	ຕາລາງເວລາ
tin opener	kheuang khăi ká-pạwng	ເຄື່ອງໄຂກະປອງ
tip (gratuity)	ngóen thip	ເງິນທິບ
tired	meuay	ເໝື່ອຍ
today	mêu-nîi	ມື້ນີ້
together	phâwm kạn	ພ້ອມກັນ
toilet	hàwng nâm	ຫ້ອງນ້ຳ
toilet paper	jîa hàwng nâm	ເຈ້ຍຫ້ອງນ້ຳ
tomorrow	mêu-eun	ມື້ອື່ນ
tonight	khéun nîi	ຄືນນີ້

too (also)	dûay	ດ້ວຍ
too (as in 'too hot')	phôht	ໂພດ
tooth	khàew	ແຂ້ວ
torch (flashlight)	fái săai	ໄຟສາຍ
to touch	jáp	ຈັບ
to tour	thawng thiaw	ທ່ອງທ່ຽວ

I'm touring Laos.
khàwy kạm-láng thawng thiaw yuu pá-thêht láo — ຂ້ອຍກຳລັງທ່ອງທ່ຽວຢູ່ປະເທດລາວ

tourist	nak thawng thiaw	ນັກທ່ອງທ່ຽວ
towards	thŏeng	ເຖິງ
towel	phàa set tọh	ຜ້າເຊັດໂຕ
town	méuang	ເມືອງ
track (path)	tháang	ທາງ
in transit	dọen tháang phaan	ເດີນທາງຜ່ານ
to translate	pạe	ແປ
translation	kạan pạe	ການແປ
trekking	dọen paa	ເດີນປ່າ
trip	thìaw	ຖ້ຽວ
true	thèuk tâwng	ຖືກຕ້ອງ
to trust	seua	ເຊື່ອ
to try (attempt)	pha-nyáa-nyáam	ພະຍາຍາມ
to try (taste food)	síim	ຊີມ
to try on (clothing)	láwng nung kheuang	ລອງໜຸ່ງເຄື່ອງ
TV	thóh-la-that	ໂທລະທັດ

U

umbrella	khán hom	ຄັນຮົ່ມ
uncomfortable	baw sá-dùak	ບໍ່ສະດວກ
under	tâi/ kâwng	ໃຕ້/ກ້ອງ

to understand	khào jại	ເຂົ້າໃຈ

I don't understand.
khàwy baw khào jại — ຂ້ອຍບໍ່ເຂົ້າໃຈ

Do you understand?
jâo khào jại baw — ເຈົ້າເຂົ້າໃຈບໍ່

unemployed	wàang ngáan	ຫວ້າງງານ
university	ma-hăa-wi-tha-nyáa-lái	ມະຫາວິທະຍາໄລ
unsafe	baw pàwt-phái	ບໍ່ປອດໄພ
until	jọn thŏeng	ຈົນເຖິງ
up	khèun	ຂຶ້ນ
upstairs	sân thóeng	ຊັ້ນເທິງ
urgent	duan	ດ່ວນ
useful	pẹn pá-nyòht	ເປັນປະໂຫຍດ
useless	baw míi pá-nyòht	ບໍ່ມີປະໂຫຍດ

V

vacation (holiday)	phak tháang kạan	ພັກທາງການ
vaccination	sak-yáa-pâwng-kạn lôhk	ຊັກຢາປ້ອງກັນໂລກ
in vain	het tae baw dâi hap phŏn	ເຮັດແຕ່ບໍ່ໄດ້ຮັບຜົນ
valuable	míi khaa	ມີຄ່າ
value	láa-kháa	ລາຄາ
various	sing taang-taang	ສິ່ງຕ່າງໆ
vegetable garden	sŭan phák	ສວນຜັກ
vegetarian (person)	khón kịn jẹh	ຄົນກິນເຈ
vegetarian (adj)	jẹh	ເຈ
very	lăai	ຫຼາຍ
video	wíi-dịi-ọh	ວີດີໂອ
view	thíu-thát	ທິວທັດ
village	muu bâan	ໝູ່ບ້ານ
visa	wi-sáa	ວີຊາ
to visit	nyîam-nyáam	ຢ້ຽມຢາມ

to vomit	hâak	ຮາກ
to vote	lêuak tâng	ເລືອກຕັ້ງ

W

to wait	láw thàa	ລໍຖ້າ

Wait a moment!
thàa béut neung ຖ້າບຶດໜຶ່ງ

waiter	dék sòep	ເດັກເສີບ
walk	nyaang	ຍ່າງ

Do you want to go for a walk?
jâo yàak pai nyaang lîin baw ເຈົ້າຢາກໄປຍ່າງ ຫຼິ້ນບ

to walk	nyaang	ຍ່າງ
to want	tâwng-kaan/yàak	ຕ້ອງການ/ຢາກ

I want ...
khàwy tâwng-kaan ... ຂ້ອຍຕ້ອງການ ...

We want ...
phûak háo tâwng-kaan ... ພວກເຮົາຕ້ອງການ ...

Do you want ...?
jâo tâwng-kaan ... baw ເຈົ້າຕ້ອງການ ... ບໍ່

war	sŏng-kháam	ສົງຄາມ
warm	óp-un	ອົບອຸ່ນ
to wash (oneself)	àap-nâm	ອາບນ້ຳ

I have to wash (bathe).
khàwy tâwng àap-nâm ຂ້ອຍຕ້ອງອາບນ້ຳ

to wash (clothes)	sak	ຊັກ
to wash (other objects)	lâang	ລ້າງ
watch	kaan duu-láe	ການດູແລ
to watch	boeng	ເບິ່ງ

Watch out!
la-wáng ລະວັງ

water	nâm	ນ້ຳ

way	tháang	ທາງ
Which way?		
tháang dạị		ທາງໃດ
WC	hàwng nâm	ຫ້ອງນ້ຳ
we	phûak háo	ພວກເຮົາ
wealthy	hang míi	ຮັ່ງມີ
weather	ạa-kàat	ອາກາດ
wedding	ngáan taeng-ngáan	ງານແຕ່ງງານ
week	ạa-thit	ອາທິດ
Welcome!		
nyín dịi tâwn hap		ຍິນດີຕ້ອນຮັບ
well	nâm sàang	ນ້ຳສ້າງ
west	thit tạa-wén tók	ທິດຕາເວັນຕົກ
wet	pìak	ປຽກ
what	nyăng	ຫຍັງ
What time is it?		
jak móhng		ຈັກໂມງ
What did you say?		
jâo wâo nyăng		ເຈົ້າເວົ້າຫຍັງ
when	wéh-láa dạị	ເວລາໃດ
where	yuu săi	ຢູ່ໃສ
who	phăi	ໃຜ
Who do I ask?		
khàwy ja thăam phăi		ຂ້ອຍຈະຖາມໃຜ
wife	mía	ເມຍ
to win	sa-na	ຊະນະ
window	pawng îam	ປ່ອງຢ້ຽມ
winter	la-dụu năo	ລະດູໜາວ
wise	hûu lăai	ຮູ້ຫຼາຍ
wish	kạan ạa-thí-thăan	ການອາທິຖານ
to wish	ạa-thí-thăan	ອາທິຖານ

with	káp	ກັບ
within	pháai-nái	ພາຍໃນ
without	pạa-sá-jàak	ປາສະຈາກ
woman	mae nyíng	ແມ່ຍິງ
wooden	het dûay mâi	ເຮັດດ້ວຍໄມ້
work	wîak	ວຽກ
to work	het wîak	ເຮັດວຽກ
world	lôhk	ໂລກ
worse (adj)	sua kwaa	ຊົ່ວກ່ວາ
worse (adv)	hâai-háeng-kwaa	ຮ້າຍແຮງກ່ວາ
write	khĭan	ຂຽນ

I'm writing ...
khàwy kạm-láng khĭan ... ຂ້ອຍກຳລັງຂຽນ ...
She's writing ...
láo kạm-láng khĭan ... ລາວກຳລັງຂຽນ ...

wrong	phít phâat	ຜິດພາດ

You're wrong.
jâo phít ເຈົ້າຜິດ

Y

year	pịi	ປີ
two years ago	sǎwng pịi kawn	ສອງປີກ່ອນ
yes	maen	ແມ່ນ
yesterday	mêu-wáan nîi	ມື້ວານນີ້
you (sg)	jâo	ເຈົ້າ
you (pl)	phûak jâo	ພວກເຈົ້າ
young	num	ໜຸ່ມ

Z

zone	khèht	ເຂດ
zoo	sŭan sát	ສວນສັດ
zodiac	hŏh-láa-sàat	ໂຫຼາສາດ

INDEX

SUSTAINABLE TRAVEL

As the climate change debate heats up, the matter of sustainability becomes an important part of the travel vernacular. In practical terms, this means assessing our impact on the environment and local cultures and economies – and acting to make that impact as positive as possible. Here are some basic phrases to get you on your way …

COMMUNICATION & CULTURAL DIFFERENCES

I'd like to learn some of your local dialects.

khâwy yàak hien pháa-sǎa	ຂ້ອຍຢາກຮຽນພາສາ
thâwng thin khǎwng jâo	ທ້ອງຖິ່ນຂອງເຈົ້າ

Would you like me to teach you some English?

jâo yàak hài khàwy sǎwn	ເຈົ້າຢາກໃຫ້ຂ້ອຍສອນ
pháa-sǎa ąng-kit hài baw	ພາສາອັງກິດໃຫ້ບໍ່

Is this a local or national custom?

nîi maen pá-phéh-nii	ນີ້ແມ່ນປະເພນີ
khǎwng thâwng thin	ຂອງທ້ອງກິ່ນ
lěu khǎwng sâat	ຫຼືຂອງຊາດ

I respect your customs.

khâwy náp-thěu	ຂ້ອຍນັບຖື
pá-phéh-nii khǎwng jâo	ປະເພນີຂອງເຈົ້າ

COMMUNITY BENEFIT & INVOLVEMENT

What sorts of issues is this community facing?

bąn-hǎa nyǎng thii	ບັນຫາຫຍັງທີ່
thâwng thin nîi	ທ້ອງຖິ່ນນີ້
kąm-láng pá-sop	ກຳລັງປະສົບ

climate and monsoon weather	phái thám-ma-sâat	ໄພທຳມະຊາດ
deforestation	kąan tát-mâi	ການຕັດໄມ້
freedom of the press	ít-sa-lá nái kąan khǐan khao sǎan	ອິສະລະໃນການ ຂຽນຂ່າວສານ

ongoing poverty	bạn-hăa khwáam nyâak jón	ບັນຫາ ຄວາມຍາກຈົນ
unemployment	kạan waang ngáan	ການຫວ່າງງານ

I'd like to volunteer my skills.
khâwy yạak ạa-săa sá-mak hét wîek — ຂ້ອຍຢາກອາສາ ສະມັກເຮັດວຽກ

Are there any volunteer programs available in the area?
mii khóhng kạan ạa-săa-sa-mák yuu thâwng thin nîi baw — ມີໂຄງການ ອາສາສະມັກ ຢູ່ທ້ອງຖິ່ນນີ້ບໍ່

ENVIRONMENT

Where can I recycle this?
khâwy khwán thîm án nîi yuu săi — ຂ້ອຍຄວນຖິ້ມ ອັນນີ້ຢູ່ໃສ

TRANSPORT

Can we get there by public transport?
khii lót dawy sạan hâwt baw — ຂີ່ລົດໂດຍສານຮອດບໍ່

Can we get there by bike?
khii lot thìip hâwt baw — ຂີ່ລົດຖີບຮອດບໍ່

I'd prefer to walk there.
khâwy já nyaang ào — ຂ້ອຍຈະຍ່າງເອົາ

ACCOMMODATION

I'd like to stay at a locally-run hotel.
khâwy yạak phak yuu hóhng háem thii khón thâwng thin bạw-li-hăan — ຂ້ອຍຢາກພັກຢູ່ ໂຮງແຮມທີ່ຄົນ ທ້ອງຖິ່ນບໍລິຫານ

Are there any ecolodges here?
mii bawn phak nái khẹht paa thám-ma-sâat baw — ມີບ່ອນພັກໃນເຂດ ປ່າທຳມະຊາດບໍ່

SUSTAINABLE TRAVEL

Can I turn the air conditioning off and open the window?

khâwy yạak mâwt ạe yẹn	ຂ້ອຍຢາກມອດແອເຢັນ
láe pŏet pawng yîam dâi baw	ແລະເປີດປ່ອງຢ້ຽມໄດ້ບໍ່

There's no need to change my sheets.

baw tâwng píen phàa	ບໍ່ຕ້ອງປ່ຽນຜ້າ
pụu bawn	ປູບ່ອນ

SHOPPING

Where can I buy locally produced goods/souvenirs?

yuu săi thii khâwy săa-mâat	ຢູ່ໃສທີ່ຂ້ອຍສາມາດ
sêu khăwng sâi/	ຊື້ຂອງໃຊ້/
thii-la-léuk thii	ທີ່ລະລຶກທີ່
khón thâwng thin hét	ຄົນທ້ອງຖິ່ນເຮັດ

Is this made from ...?	nîi maen hét jạak ... baw	ນີ້ແມ່ນເຮັດ ຈາກ ... ບໍ່
deer antlers	khăo kwạang	ເຂົາກວາງ
elephant tusks	ngáa sâang	ງາຊ້າງ
snake skin	năng ngúu	ຫນັງງູ
tiger skin	năng sĕua	ຫນັງເສືອ

FOOD

Do you sell ...?	jâo khăai ...	ເຈົ້າຂາຍ ...
locally produced food	phá-lít-ta-phán ạa-hăan khăwng thâwng thin baw	ຜລິດຕະພັນ ອາຫານຂອງ ທ້ອງຖິ່ນບໍ່
organic produce	phá-lít-ta-phán baw mii săan khéh-mii baw	ຜລິດຕະພັນ ບໍ່ມີສານ ເຄມີບໍ່

Can you tell me which traditional foods I should try?

ạa-hăan phêun méuang dăi	ອາຫານພື້ນເມືອງໃດ
thii khâwy khwán síim	ທີ່ຂ້ອຍຄວນຊີມ

SIGHTSEEING

Does your	bạw-li-sát	ບໍລິສັດ
company ...?	khǎwng thaan ...	ຂອງທ່ານ ...
donate money	bạw-li-jàak	ບໍລິຈາກ
to charity	ngóen hài	ເງິນໃຫ້
	sá-thǎan-thii	ສະຖານທີ່
	sǒng kháw baw	ສົງເຄາະບໍ່
hire local	jâang phûu	ຈ້າງຜູ້
guides	nám thiaw jàak	ນຳທ່ຽວຈາກ
	thâwng thin baw	ທ້ອງຖິ່ນບໍ່
visit local	yîam yạam	ຢ້ຽມຢາມ
businesses	bán-dạa	ບັນດາ
	thú-la-kít	ທຸລະກິດ
	thâwng thin baw	ທ້ອງຖິ່ນບໍ້
Does the guide	phûu nám thiaw	ຜູ້ນຳທ່ຽວ
speak ...?	wâo pháa-sǎa ... baw	ເວົ້າພາສາ ... ບໍ່
Karen	ká-lieng	ກະຫລ່ຽງ
Mong	mông	ມົ້ງ
Thaidam	thái dạm	ໄທດຳ
Vientiane	láo wiéng-jạn	ລາວວຽງຈັນ
Yao	yâo	ຢ້າວ

Are cultural tours available?

mii kạan thawng thiaw	ມີການທ່ອງທ່ຽວ
wát-thá-ná-thám baw	ວັດທະນະທຳບໍ້

lonely planet
don't just stand there,
say something!
o see the full range of our language products, go to:
lonelyplanet.com

Lonely Planet Offices

Australia
90 Maribyrnong St, Footscray,
Victoria 3011
☎ 03 8379 8000
fax 03 8379 8111
✉ talk2us@lonelyplanet.com.au

USA
150 Linden St, Oakland,
CA 94607
☎ 510 893 8555
fax 510 893 8572
✉ info@lonelyplanet.com

UK
2nd floor, 186 City Rd
London EC1V 2NT
☎ 020 7106 2100
fax 020 7106 2101
✉ go@lonelyplanet.co.uk